Up My Personal Effectiveness

For maximum Personal and Team Impact

Jonathan Chua

ISBN: 978-981-14-5616-9

Published by OnePurpleTree

Block 3016, EASTech #08-04, Bedok North Ave 4, Singapore 489947

www.onepurpletree.com

Up My Core Skills Series

To my angel, Angela

CONTENTS

Introduction

It is a fundamental assumption and belief of this book that everyone wants to be effective and to be able to make positive personal and team impact. Each one has the capacity to do so. These provide the basis for this learning.

Let's begin this learning by asking a question: "What is Personal Effectiveness really? What are some thoughts or pictures that come to your mind when you ask this question?" As much as money means many things to many people, and success means different things to different people, so can responses to this question be very diverse. In fact if you were to ask 100 people what is Personal Effectiveness, you will probably get 107 definitions.

Fully aware of this challenge, I shall not attempt to make any exclusive nor authoritative definition for Personal Effectiveness. That's not the objective of this book. It is necessary, however, to have a definition for this conversation to be meaningful. This book shall refer Personal Effectiveness as the effort one takes to achieve his or her goals in a focused manner that ensures optimum results. It could involve committing one's energy, time and resources to identifying the skill-sets and tool-sets required to accomplish the goals. These shall be our guiding points for discussion. Readers will learn to identify his personal resources, determine his goals, and develop an action plan to achieve these goals. Readers will pick up necessary tool-sets and hone essential skill-sets to help him achieve goals effectively.

This book explores achieving personal effectiveness for maximum personal and team impact through 3 main thoughts and is divided into 4 parts. The 3 main thoughts are developing a resilience Mindset, honing necessary Skill-set, and equipping with essential Tool-set to Up My Personal Effectiveness.

In Part 1, personal effectiveness is likened to someone planning on a journey. It helps one to discover the current position and resources, and encourages one to develop worthy goals. Part 1 ends off encouraging one to develop a success and resilience mindset.

Part 2 begins with a caution that a great plan does not guarantee success and that the aim of an action plan is meant for action not documentation! It then gets into quick gear on developing an action plan for personal effectiveness. Tools and helps to develop the personal action plan are explored here. Obstacles to action plan are discussed and suggestions to overcome them explored.

Part 3 shares useful skills that would help increase personal effectiveness. Time management and stress management skills are discussed. Time wasters, when left unchecked, can easily offset your effectiveness. Stresses creep in uninvited when one is pursuing goals and sabotage successes. Self-motivation skill is essential to keep one going on when things get on bumpy patches.

Part 4 explores the skills necessary for working with others. Effective communication skill is key to help human to work effectively as powerful teams. Conflict resolution skill allows us to live harmoniously in community. These 2 skills allow us to overcome animals that are physically faster and more powerful than us, and to survive in harsh uninhabitable environments.

This book aims to allow you to look into the mirror at the end of each day and honestly say: "It has been a great day! I have been accountable for the resources gifted me."

A clarification to note. All characters mentioned in this book, minus those in the 4-minutes mile, are fictitious and are created to illustrate or emphasise a point. Any resemblances to anyone you

Introduction

know are purely coincidental.

May I wish you a great exploring to Up My Personal Effectiveness for maximum personal and team impact.

www.onepurpletree.com

PART ONE

Understand Personal Effectiveness

Develop a Success Mindset.

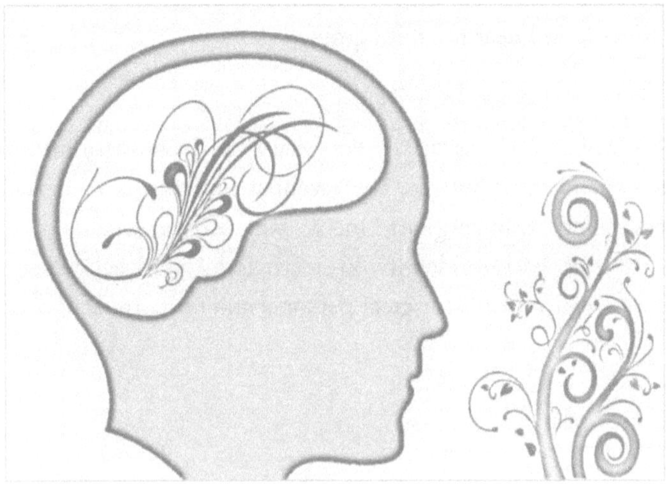

Some people seem to be able to accomplish pretty much what they said they would do. They are very clear about their goals. They appeared confident, well managed and well resourced. They would usually head the chart of successful lists and cited for their accomplishments. News media love to seek their comments, and magazines like to feature them.

Some other people seem to struggle just to be in the mentioned lists. They are not organised and seem to be in need most of the time. Their visions and goals are not well articulated. Some of the times they made it into the list, other times they do not. They are not the person you would go to for advice and help.

Then there is the rest of the crowd. Their faces are in a blur, and we don't take notice of them. We don't realise that they existed. They are around just to form an existential background.

While we can easily identify some of those people in the first category, it is not difficult to figure out the rest of the people in the third group too. We may put ourselves in the second category conveniently, or just to avoid a cruel self-reflection. Secretly hoping not to be found near the third group.

This need not be the case.

Each one of us can Up My Personal Effectiveness for maximum personal and team impact. The essential first step is to develop a success mindset. In this Part One we will discover what is personal effectiveness, how to identify one's strengths and weaknesses, and employ effective tools for great personal and team impact.

Chapter 1

Personal Effectiveness and its Applications

Personal effectiveness refers to the efforts one takes to achieve his or her goals in a focused manner that ensure optimum results. It involves committing one's energy, time and resources to identifying the skill-sets and tool-sets required to accomplish the goals.

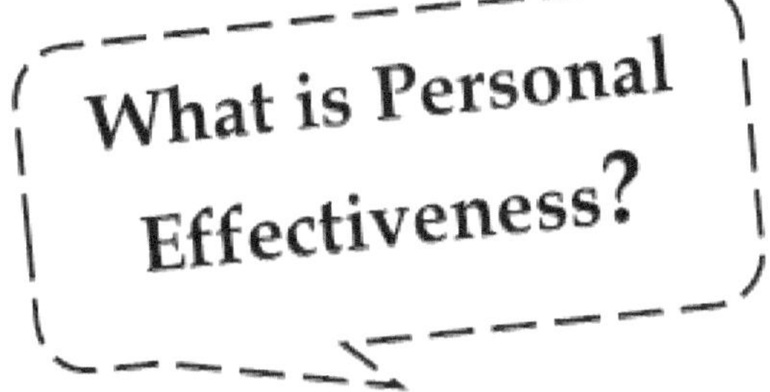

Let's unpack this. There are goals (personal and/or work) a person is working toward. This person seeks to use his resources (personal and professional, existing and future) to achieve these identified goals. Personal Effectiveness is the honing of essential skills, the utilization of one's resources, both personal and professional, to achieve desired goals.

Effectiveness and Efficiency

There is a common confusion as regards to personal effectiveness. Effectiveness is commonly mixed up with efficiency. While they are close cousins, these two are not quite the same. They are however usually found together and in most cases, complement and support each other. Thus the common mixed up. This is not a play of words, but efficiency is about doing the thing right and effectiveness is doing the right thing. These are quite different and distinct skills. We would consider both in Up My Personal Effectiveness.

Efficiency is how fast you can complete a task or a job. For example if most of us take one hour to clean up a living room and you take only half an hour to clean up that same room, then you are two times more efficient than the rest of us. It is a measure of the speed a task is done or how quickly a task can be accomplished. Another example is if one machine is able to produce 100 pieces of cake in an hour, and another machine is able to produce 300 pieces of the same cake in an hour. Then the second machine is 3 times more efficient than the first one. Some refer this to productivity.

Effectiveness however, does not concern with throughput or how fast a task is completed. For example if one had a fever and he took a particular medicine, and the fever left him. Then that medicine is effective to relieve fever. That medicine did the job it was designed to do. If after taking the medicine and the fever did not subside back to normal body temperature, then that medicine is not effective. It did not accomplish what it was supposed to do.

Personal Effectiveness is Liken on a Journey

Let's say you plan to get on a journey. You want to get from point A to point B. The following steps are probably how to go about the planning. The first task is to chart out the path from A to B. Then to identify any obstacle or unique features along this path. There may be a stretch of paved road that we can travel by car, a river that needs to be crossed, a distant of country dirt road, and a little hill in its path. After identifying these situations we need to equip ourselves with relevant tools and skills to overcome them. With these done can we then be successful in reaching our destination.

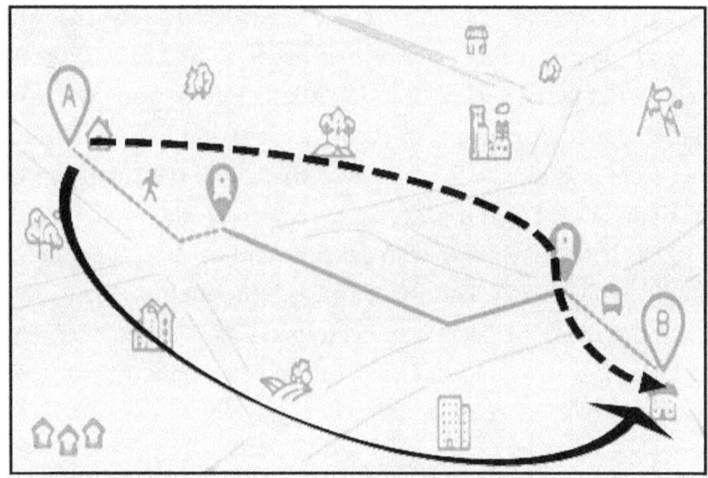

Learning Effectiveness from Planning a Journey

Now let's liken Personal Effectiveness to be planning for a journey. There is a clearly defined endpoint (point B) that you want to go to. So point B is your desired goal, the destination you want to reach. There is a starting point (point A) where you are right now. Point A is your current situation. And then there is a planned path of getting from point A to point B. This path shall be your Action Plan, detailing the necessary actions required to get you to the desired goals. Along the way, there are some checkpoints to track your progress and ascertain your orientation. You may need to pick up some effectiveness tools and develop effectiveness skills to help you reach your goals.

The Need for Personal Effectiveness

Personal effectiveness gets you to your destination with comfort and ease. That is, it helps you accomplish what you set out to do, and sets you on the road to assured successes.

Let us continue with the previous example. For example along the path from Point A to Point B, we have identified the following: a stretch of paved road, a river that needs to be crossed, another stretch of country dirt road, and a little hill in its path. We would need some tools and skills to ensure a successful journey. We may need a car or a bicycle for the paved road, with the corresponding skill to drive a car or ride a bicycle. Sure, you can choose to walk this distance. It will likely take a longer time and be more strenuous to complete this stretch. This is a choice of efficiency. We may need a raft, and acquire the necessary skill to paddle across the river. Then get hold of a 4-wheel-drive jeep to cross the country road. And finally, the skill and equipment to climb the hill.

This simple journey of getting from Point A to Point B turns out to be quite involved. But with the necessary tools and the respective skills to handle these tools properly, you would be able to successfully reach your Point B (effective) with comfort and ease (efficient).

The need for personal effectiveness can be likened to the need to sharpen your saw and upgrading your skills. For the saw to be effective cutting down a tree, you want to maintain and ensure its sharpness. A blunt saw just wouldn't do the job. If you persisted the cutting with the blunt saw, you would need to put in much more effort and end up with much frustration and an unsatisfactory job. Perhaps damage the saw along the way.

Tools improve both our efficiency and effectiveness. For example we need to drive a nail into the wall. Try imagining us trying to push the nail into the wall with our bare hands. It will be such a frustration, and a bloody failure. I will not suggest you try this even if you are a karate expert. A hammer will easily get the job done with ease and comfort. If however we need to open a can of food, a hammer wouldn't be of great help. It would mess up the job. For this instance, we would need a can opener to do the job.

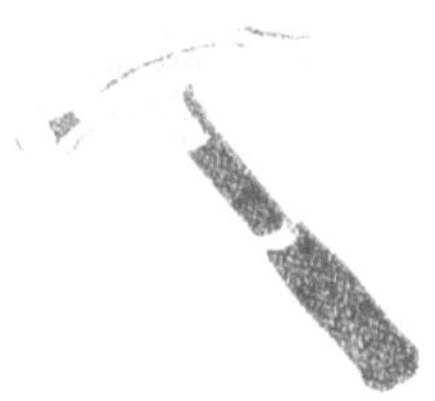

If we only have a hammer however, we would treat every job to be like a nail. That would be rather messy if not destructive. Equipped with the right tool for the right job allows us to be effective. Having the right tool for the right job is important.

Personal effectiveness allows you to accomplish your goals with ease and comfort. To up your personal effectiveness, you would need to know the essential tools and skill-sets, when and how to apply them accordingly.

Improve Personal Effectiveness

To better your personal effectiveness, you can take the following actions:

1) Take time to first reflect on your current situations.

2)   Next to determine your desired goals.

3)   Then to develop an actionable plan.

It is like taking on a journey. You need to first determine where your current location is. Next is to determine where you want to go (setting goals). The actionable plan is likened to charting the journey on the map which helps you navigate and tracks its progress to your destination.

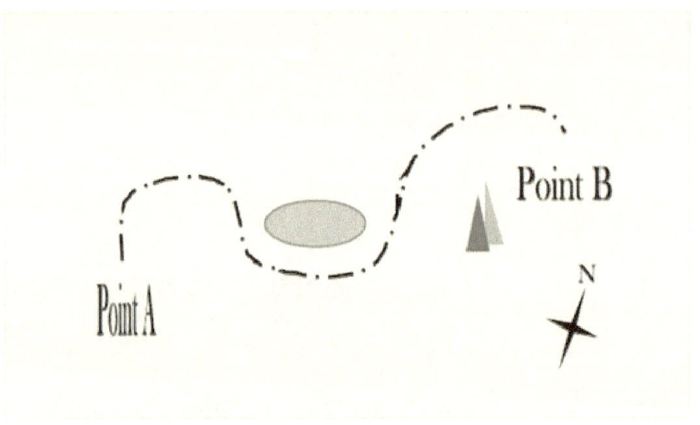

Action 1 'to reflect on current situations' will be covered in Part One, and Actions 2 and 3 will be covered in Part Two of this book.

We can break down these 3 actions into more detailed steps.

1.   Identifying what is really important and what you really want to accomplish, something you will be committed to achieving. This is goal setting, determining the destination.

2.   Identifying your values, and reflecting if you are currently living in alignment with the identified goals.

3.   Identifying where and how you are spending your time and resources, and checking if these are in line with your values and goals.

Steps 2 and 3 are identifying your current situations.

4. Drawing out an Action Plan. This is planning the journey. Identifying what tools you might need and what skills would be helpful to get you to the goals.

5. Asking for feedback from people you trust. This helps to identify your blind spots. They could also help in keeping you on track and motivated. These people can help to hold you accountable.

Chapter 2

Personal Strengths and Weaknesses

Each one of us has our strengths and intelligence. Even the strong and successful people have their weaknesses. They are just good at playing to their strength, and not exposing their weaknesses. Some of us have clearly identified and are aware of our strengths and weaknesses. Some are yet to discover their hidden talents. Knowing your own strengths and intelligence could help you leverage on them for maximum effect and impact in your life. Identifying your weaknesses allows you to work on them, to overcome their limitations and limits their effects on your performance.

There are a few ways and tools to identify our strengths and weaknesses. We can use some tools available in the market. Some of them are free and well tested. SWOT and SOAR analyses are some common tools. Other commercial tools require a fee to get the analysis done. Some examples include EQ-I 2.0 Emotional Intelligence Assessment, Wiley's DiSC product, WorkPlace Big 5, VIA®Me! and Kolbe Index Test.

An example of an online aptitude test:

Free Aptitude Test – RichardStep Strengths and Weaknesses Aptitude Test (RSWAT)

This tool allows you to get a better look at who you really are and how much you could grow.

http://richardstep.com/richardstep-strengths-weaknesses-aptitude-test/

One quick and direct way to identify our strengths and weaknesses is to ask some people whom we trust to give us feedback. It may be helpful to give them some guides (or prepared questions) on how to provide us true and honest feedback. A simplified SWOT questionnaire should solicit good feedback.

SWOT Analysis

SWOT Analysis or sometimes known as SWOT matrix, is a well-established and straight forward technique to provide a snapshot of a current situation.

SWOT stands for Strengths, Weaknesses, Opportunities, and Threats.

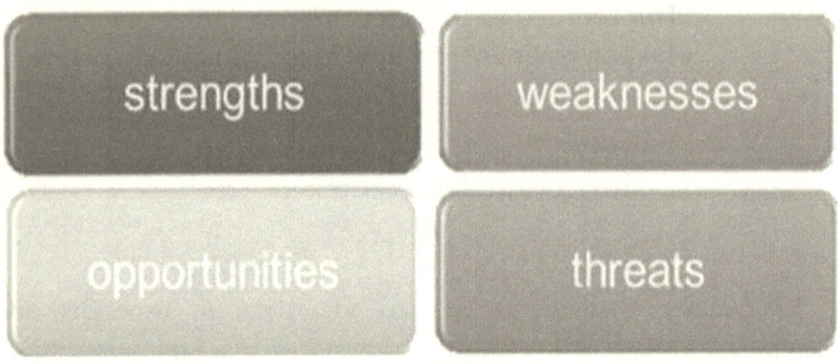

This matrix aims to help organisation or individuals identify one's STRENGTHS (resources, capabilities), WEAKNESSES (deficiencies, negative traits), OPPORTUNITIES (positive economic trends, unique favourable conditions), and THREATS (potential harmful trends, situations that expose your weakness). While organisations may use it as a strategic tool to plot out their next phase of planning, individuals may use it to improve their personal effectiveness.

SWOT matrix allows a business or individual to have a quick analysis of its present situation and use that as a starting point for planning.

Conducting a SWOT Analysis

One can begin the SWOT analysis by asking some questions in each of the four areas to be examined. Be as truthful as possible for a meaningful result. Be as detailed as you can be. It is okay not to have all the answers. Getting feedback from someone you trust can be very helpful too. Below are just some examples of the question to help you get started with SWOT analysis.

Strengths

- What do you do well?
- What do others see as your strengths?
- What skills have you worked to develop?

Weaknesses

- What are your negative work habits and traits?
- What could you improve?
- What are others likely to see as your weaknesses?

Opportunities

- What is the state of the economy/situation?
- What trends could you take advantage of?
- How can you turn your strengths into opportunities?

Threats

- What threats do your weaknesses expose you to?
- What trends could harm you?

You can check this link regarding
conducting a Personal SWOT

https://www.mindtools.com/pages/article/
newTMC_05_1.htm

Chapter 3

Develop a Success Mindset

4-Minutes Mile

4-minute mile run was thought to be impossible. They argued that the human body is not designed to run a mile under 4 minutes. Some even suggested that it was dangerous to do so. For many years (some claimed thousand years, I am unable to confirm this) no one could do a 4-minute mile. It was accepted as a physiological limit for the human being.

Then in 1954, Roger Bannister broke the 4-minute barrier, running the distance in 3:59.4. In the next one year, some more runners beat the 4-minutes mile. Now, the 4-minute mile is no longer the target, it is the norm. The current record holder is Hicham El Guerrouj, who ran a time of 3:43.13 in Rome in 1999. We can be fairly sure that this shall not be the final record - someone is sure to break this again. Now we know that 4-minutes mile was a psychological limit. Once someone demonstrated that it can be done, everyone else seems to be able to do it.

It Is a Mindset

It was said that Roger Bannister trained himself to visualise the achievement during his training, to create a sense of certainty in his mind and body. He did it by changing the mindset, rejecting the claim that it cannot be done. So, Roger broke the 4-minute mile in his mind first before he did it in reality.

So can each one of us.

Well, I am not referring to the 4-minute mile. I'd like to propose that each one of us has the capability and can up our personal effectiveness, to see ourselves more successful in whatever we will to do. We need first to adjust our mindset for success.

Face of a Success Mindset

A success mindset is accepting the fact that we can be successful in what we will to do. The definition of success is not to be in the number one top spot. If it happens to be, that's fine. Success is achieving what one viewed as valuable and will to achieve it, having an action plan to work toward that goal, and is making progress along that path. It has nothing to do with competing with someone else. It is not comparing with another person. Success is about the process of accomplishing what you set out to do.

In Part Two of Up My Personal Effectiveness -- "Develop Action Plan", we will explore the steps from developing a success mindset to executing the success plan. Just before we proceed to Part Two to develop an action plan, let's discuss the importance of setting goal.

Set Worthy Goal

While honing essential self-management tools could get you to be more effective and efficient in your daily dealings, it is most critical to determine your worthy goal. Without a clear worthy goal, that could be likened to have upgraded your four wheels drive vehicle with an enhanced efficient engine and extra power, going on a journey with a map but without an established destination. You do not want to be effective and efficient running up the wrong mountain! This is like a headless bull on steroid charging aimlessly with no specific target. The bull will end up in the wrong place. If this situation is not deemed dangerous, it can only at best be entirely meaningless. Try to imagine driving a car with no specific destination, and going round and round about with no end. With no destination to go you will always end up nowhere. This is an absolute total waste of time and effort.

A simple diagram helps to show that when a wrong goal is chosen, it will definitely lead to frustration. It is only a matter of how soon that will happen. When the right goals are determined, effective and efficient tools and skills will get you to fulfillment! But with low

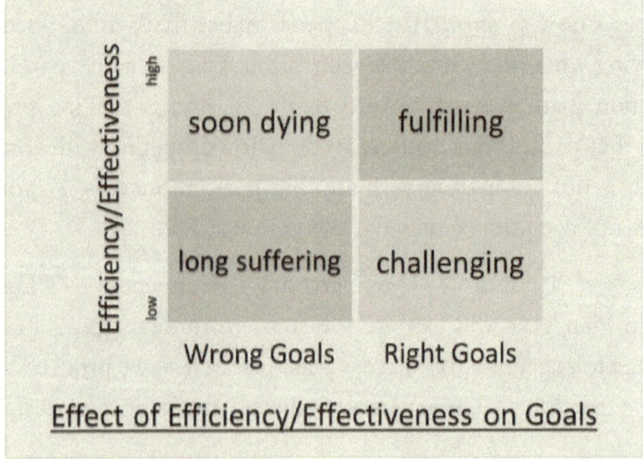

Effect of Efficiency/Effectiveness on Goals

efficiency and non-effective tools, achieving right goals become challenging. With wrong goals however, the final outcomes can range from soon dying to slow dying or disappointment, depending on whether you've got the right tools. In these cases effective tools will get you to disappointment sooner.

Take as an example a worthy goal of setting up a community garden where the neighbourhood can participate and enjoy. With the relevant knowledge and skills of gardening, and equipped with the right tools, the community garden could be realized soon for all to enjoy, admire and interact. However, without the knowledge, skills and tools, it would take quite a while to fulfill this dream. The process can also become rather unpleasant and long-suffering when neighbours begin to complain about the dirt, noise, mosquitos and inconveniences. Take deforestation as a quick consideration of wrong goal and its effects. With modern motorized machines we have quicken its pace of destruction.

It is critical to spend some time to determine what is really important to you and set that as your worthy goal.

We will look into setting worthy goals in Part Two – Develop Action Plan.

PART TWO

Develop Action Plan

Equip with Necessary Tool-Sets

Chen Gong has always knew that he wanted to be successful. Since young he has visualised a successful life. Starting a hugely profitable business by age 35, doing social goods, helping many people find meaningful jobs, inspiring young aspiring entrepreneurs. And yet having plenty of time to pursue his passion to travel around the world. He has been passionate about these dreams and seriously hoping to turn them into reality.

These dreams have been brewing for the last 30 years, and Chen Gong is now 50 years old. He has yet to achieve any of his dreams. What happened! Or rather, what did not happen?

There is a huge gap between knowing what you want to do and doing what you know. The "knowing" may get you to the starting point, the "doing" is essentially crucial to your reaching the desired destination. You need both the knowing and the doing to get to your goal. Deficiency in any of these will not get you near your desired goal.

After discovering your excitable dreams, it is critical to develop an action plan to realise them. If not they will remain at best only as dreams. The action plan clarifies your goals and set up the path to achieving them. It identifies any tools and skills that are required to achieve these goals. If you do not already have these skills, it would serve you well to acquire them sooner.

Developing an Action Plan is not exactly a walk in the park, neither is executing it. They require much effort.

In this Part Two of Develop Action Plan: Equip with Necessary Tool-Sets, we will discover how to bridge the gap between knowing and doing, thereby ensuring a successful achieving of your worthy goals. Many useful planning tools will be discussed in Part Two.

Chapter 4

Essential Planning Tools for Action Plan

Goal Setting

Goal setting is the process of establishing an objective or goal that you will to achieve. It has to be measurable and with a timeframe to accomplish it. Some call this timeframe the deadline. There are few elements to that statement that deserve a closer look. First there is a goal or objective to be achieved. This goal is quantifiable and can be measured. There is also a timeframe to accomplish that goal. That is, there is a validity date to achieve it. These elements need to be clearly defined so that you could tell if the goal has been accomplished or not. For example you set a goal to be healthy. This goal statement is not well written as it is not quantifiable, not measurable and has no timeframe. It lacks clarity. You would not know if or when this goal has been reached. A good example of a goal statement could look like this: To be able to climb up 10 flights of stairs without stopping in 3 months' time. You may check this goal statement against the guidelines of the SMART goal setting, which will be discussed soon.

Why are these merely a wish-list and not a goal?

The reason for goal setting

Goal setting allows you to allocate and focus your resources on achieving your desired goal or objective. It gives a clear direction as you build up your essential disciplines. It helps you to be purposeful and effective in your activities and efforts.

When you aim the arrow at nothing, you will always hit it. To achieve nothing is pretty effortless, though not always enjoyable. An aimless drift is a sure way to ineffectiveness and failure. Even for shadow boxing, a boxer needs an imaginary target to focus on for the training to be effective. Though he is effectively punching into the air, the imaginary target helps him focus and direct his punches, harnessing the relevant muscles and improving his skills.

Goal setting also provides you a motivation to move toward the objective. It provides a system to track and measure your progress. And if you are not progressing as planned, it gives you an opportunity to re-adjust and re-align your strategy to get back on track. A consecutive series of goal setting and achieving them sets you in the positive direction of successful and meaningful living.

SMART Goal Setting

A good goal statement can take the form of an acronym SMART. It provides a structure and guidance to set a goal statement. It is easy to use and does not require specialist tools or training. It is an effective tool and helps you set meaningful goal statements quickly. The following are some questions and pointers to help you get started with your SMART goal setting.

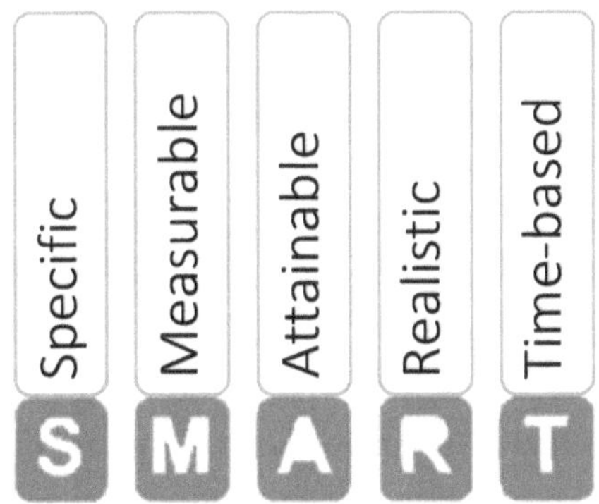

Specific

- What exactly do you want to achieve? State with clarity and in detail. It should have the "what, who, why, where"
- Example:

- Bad: I want to be healthy
- Good: I want to lose weight.

Measurable

- You need to be able to track the progress and measure the outcome. It should have the "how much or how many". It should allow you to know when it is accomplished.
- Example: I want to lose 10 kg.

Attainable

- The goal should be achievable with your skills and abilities. It should answer the "how".
- Bad example: I want to swim across the Pacific Ocean.
- Good: I want to lose 10 kg by swimming 3 times a week.

Realistic

- The goal should be achievable with your resources and time.
- Bad example: I want to lose 10 kg by tomorrow.
- Good: I want to lose 10 kg by swimming 3 times a week for 30 min each time.

Time-based

- The goal should have a deadline, it should answer the "by when".
- Example: I want to lose 10 kg by the end of the year.

With these guidelines, a SMART goal statement could be "I want to lose 10 kg by the end of the year, by swimming 3 times a week for 30 minutes each time." Compare that statement with "I want to be healthy" and it becomes clear which statement would be effective.

SOAR Analysis

SOAR analysis is a strategic planning tool that identifies one's current strengths and works on the future desired or aspired goals. The acronym stands for Strengths, Opportunities, Aspirations and

Results. SOAR's approach differs from the more commonly used SWOT analysis. SOAR focuses on current strengths and aspires to future potentials. It is a forward-looking and solution-focused strategic planning tool.

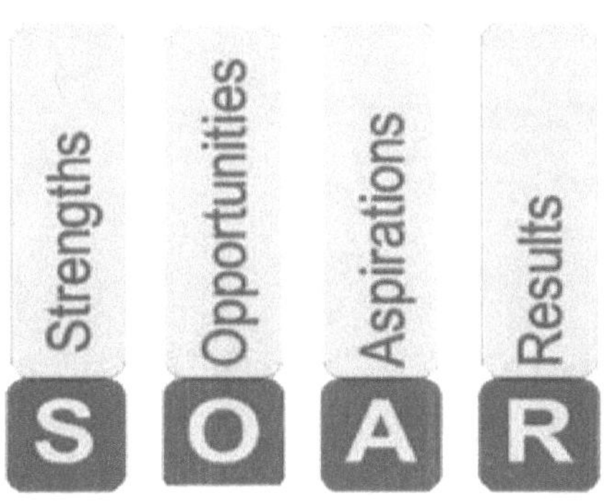

The following questions could help you conduct a SOAR analysis fairly quickly.

Strengths

- What advantages do you have?
- What do you do well?
- What unique resources do you have access to?
- What do others see as your strength?
- What factors are helping you succeed?
- Why are others helping you?

Opportunities

- Where are some good opportunities facing you?
- What partnerships might you develop?
- What are the interesting trends you are aware of?

Aspirations

- How will you build on and expand your strengths?
- What improvements do you want to see?
- Where will you be in 3 to 5 years?
- What capacities will you have?
- How do you want others to perceive you?

Results

- What difference will you make?
- What does success look like?
- What measures of success will be most important?

Compare SWOT and SOAR Analysis

The acronym SWOT stands for Strengths, Weaknesses, Opportunities and Threats. You may refresh on this analysis in Part One of this book.

SWOT Analysis	SOAR Approach
Analysis Oriented	Action Oriented
Weakness and Threat focus	Strengths and Opportunities focus
Competition focus- be better	Possibility focus- be the best
Focus on analysis- planning	Focus on planning- implementation
Attention to gaps	Attention to results

Both SWOT and SOAR are good self-analysis tools. They help you identify your strengths and weaknesses quickly, and set some aspiring goals to work on. While each has its own features and uniqueness, they have some converging similarities. They can work independently or together according to your intentions.

Gantt Chart

A Gantt chart is one of the most common and useful ways of showing activities displayed against time. It is a popular tool for project management. It is also appropriate for effective objective monitoring and achieving. The left column of the chart is a list of activities to be accomplished. The top row is the time scale against each activity targeted for completion. Each activity is represented by a bar. The starting position of the bar indicates the start date for the activity, the length of the bar indicates the duration allocated for the activity, and the end position of the bar indicates the end date for the activity. The chart also indicates the start and end dates of the whole project.

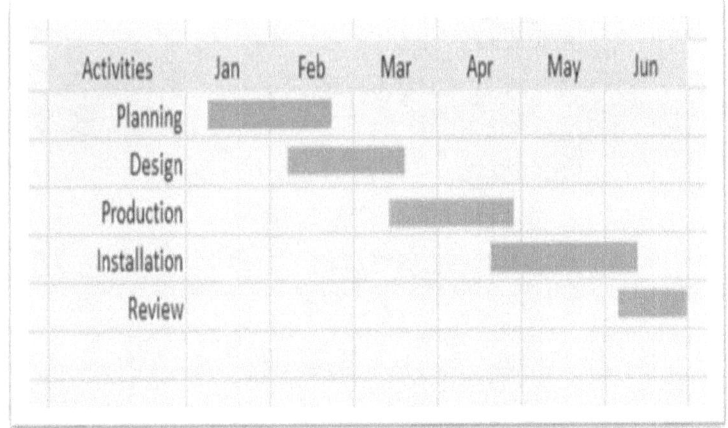

An Illustration of a Gantt chart

Goal-Setting Tools

Goal setting tools can come in the form of worksheets or templates. Generally they should be simple to use, with time frame scales and allows progress tracking and monitoring of achievement. Some examples of goal setting worksheets and templates can include "The Smart Goals Worksheet", "Your 101 Life Goals List". You can find these templates and more on-line. There are other on-line goal setting tools as well. These allow dynamic planning and monitoring for your goals. Some of these on-line goal setting tools can include "Goal-Buddy", "Goalscape".

Some goal setting worksheets and templates can be found here:

http://www.smart-goals-guide.com/free-goal-setting-worksheets-forms-and-templates.html

Some on-line goal setting tools can be found here:

https://www.thebalance.com/tools-to-help-with-your-goals-2951861

Chapter 5

Obstacles to Action Plan and Ways to Overcome Them

Setting goal is the first step toward personal effectiveness. Achieving them is the crucial next step. Between the first step and the next may not be smooth sailing nor a matter of course. Obstacles would soon surface themselves, impeding each step. It can be most challenging especially during the initial phases. Being aware of these obstacles can help you better prepared to overcome them, and successfully achieving your goals.

Now let face this 'obstacle' squarely before we get on to some common obstacles to action plan. What is an obstacle? An obstacle refers to something, material or nonmaterial that interferes with or prevents action or progress of a desired goal. It can be as literal as a wall in your path, or as intangible as a lack of imagination.

Let not the definition of obstacle obstructs us from moving along further. What are some obstacles that can jeopardise our plan?

Factors Affecting Achievement of Action Plan

The following are some common obstacles to achieving your goals.

Negative mindset, attitudes or beliefs.

ShiBai has always thought he would not make it to the football team. He had been rejected last year and the year before. So this year he did not even turn up at the selection trial. He is expecting to be rejected again. Why even try when you are sure to be rejected again? Anyway there is no big deal to be in the team.

Past failures and bad experiences could develop into a negative mindset and fatality attitudes. These could come in the form of negative self-talk and/or poor self-image. When one can only see negative outcomes, why would he even take any step forward?

Lack of focus.

TaiDuo is an ambitious girl. She is talented, has many great plans and many worthy dreams that she wants to achieve before she reaches 25. While she was studying for her master degree in financial engineering, she started her social enterprise to help the needy in a third world country. She also volunteers some of the evenings in a local community outreach to help disadvantaged students with their studies, and gets involved in an eco-sustainability activity on the weekends. She is currently working on a business proposal for a recycling project.

While it is admirable that she is involved in many worthy causes, it is apparent that TaiDuo is not really enjoying all her activities. More importantly, she is struggling to manage these goals and not doing well in any of them.

When there are too many things on the plate, the focus can become a challenge. Trying to achieve too much with limited resources can be self-defeating. Unable to prioritize goals could lead to unfocused effort and distraction, with failure as the sure outcome. At best only mediocre results for some of the attempts.

Procrastination.

Mr Deng has a favourite line: "I will get this done first thing the next morning. I promise." Very often projects that were assigned to him many weeks ago would receive this same reply 2 days after the deadline. Regardless of the urgency or importance of tasks assigned to him, this reply is pretty consistent.

All colleagues, friends and family members are beginning to take note of this pattern, not without least contempt. They are beginning to dismiss and write off Mr Deng. While he notices this change in attitude from them and knows what needed to be done, Mr Deng has already plan to do something about it tomorrow. Really!

The challenge to Mr Deng is a common one for most people. Mere laziness and lax attitude cause one to postpone important activities beyond the deadline until they become crises.

Bad time management.

XiaoLuan is still frantically trying to finalise the document format for her project report. Should she use font size 11 or 12 for the title? Should she use line spacing 1.15 or 1.5 for the main document? She has been trying out various font sizes and spacing for the last 2 hours! She has even printed some hardcopy samples for visual inspection. XiaoLuan needs to submit her proposal by 2359 tonight. She has yet to draft out the main arguments for her proposal. And yes, she has yet to select the pictures for the power-point slides!

Unable to distinguish the important activities from the urgent ones, spending too much time on non-important activities, leaving and keep postponing the critical ones lead to bad time management, often resulting in unsatisfactory if not catastrophic outcomes.

Lack of support.

At this year's annual national athletic meet, Dash came in 6th in the 100-meter race. He was expected to be among the podium finishers. Yet 2 months leading to the race, Dash had to practise in the football field as the practice track was under maintenance. The teacher-in-charge was not available to help him secure any training venue as he was busy preparing the drama team for an oversea performance. So Dash has to submit his race admin, went for the time trials, and competed in the final, all by himself.

Not getting support either in the form of emotional encouragement or material resources can sabotage the outcome.

Fail to take action.

The prospect and consequences of failure have prevented Ben from venturing into the new market. While a good business case has been built and the proposal was ready for submission to the board, Ben hesitated as it would mean a huge financial commitment to the business. And if the new venture does not work out as planned, the loss would have a great hit on the current business. Ben decided he needed more research and information before making a decision, and would wait for a better timing to make the move.

Ben did not take up the opportunity. We can only speculate on the possible outcome. Fear of failure could incapacitate one to inaction. This could be related to a negative mindset or beliefs.

Strategies to Overcome Obstacles

Obstacles are meant to be overcome and not to keep us down. With appropriate preparation, planning, tools and skills, there are strategies to overcoming them and to achieving goals. The following steps can be helpful to do that.

Step One: Build a plan.

Nobody in one's right mind would plan to fail. The common fatal error is a failure to plan. When one has the intent and plan to stay healthy, he would begin to eating right, exercising regularly and drinking plenty of water. These could begin with a conscious effort, but would soon become a part of a routine. He would end up more trim and alert, and on his way to achieving his goal. Without a clear intention and plan, no concerted effort would take place. It would probably remain as a dream, a wish.

Work out an action plan that provides a direction and focuses on achieving the goals. Refer to Chapters 4 and 6 for some planning tools.

Step Two: Break the goal into smaller chunks.

Grand goal can sound daunting and appears unachievable. For the first time goal setter, trying to achieve a goal could seem to be overwhelming too. One would not know how to begin, less about achieving these goals. For example: "I want to travel around the world when I retire!" Some immediate questions that beg a response could be when is your retirement? How will you define retirement? For how long will you travel? Which country will you begin? How many or which countries would be included for counting as the world? Such a goal statement could be daunting, and you probably do not have all the answers.

Break goals into small manageable and achievable goals. This helps in visualizing goals in smaller targets with a shorter time frame and experiencing small victories along the way. The goal becomes achievable. Take the example of completing a marathon. This would seem impossible for one who is not an exercise freak at his first attempt. Break it down into small achievable goals and work toward the completion. First aim to complete the 10 km, then go onto the 20 km, then 30 km, and finally the full marathon. The Grand goal becomes manageable with this simple strategy.

Step Three: Track progress.

After placing a piece of marinated meat on the grill over the charcoal fire, one does not just leave it there and tend to other activities. It would soon be burnt and become another piece of charcoal. If you want a great piece of BBQ steak, stay there to watch over the fire, monitor its progress and inspect the cooking. Flip it over at appropriate times, add a little flavours and seasoning when necessary. Constantly tracking its progress until it is finally ready for serving.

It is the same when working on a goal. If you desire a great outcome and success, tracking and monitoring its progress is critical. One can't just leave it to chances. Tracking progress keeps one on the toes and be responsive to the challenges along the way. Close monitoring also keeps one excited about achieving the goals.

Step Four: Celebrate small successes.

Everyone loves to be in the winning team. There is this magic and attraction that success emits. People like to be involved with and associated to a winning and successful team. Celebration evokes a sense of winning and success, thereby increases the motivation to achieve and to win even more. This kicks off a series of successes that raise morale and become unstoppable once the momentum is built.

Each progress and success, no matter how great or small deserves a celebration. These celebrations provide a sense of progress and achievement. The celebration needs not be elaborative nor glamorous with a big budget. Celebration can be simple and yet meaningful. A simple meal for a pep talk or a 5-minutes celebration cheer to mark each progress could be elevating and motivating.

Step Five: Go public about your goals.

Double07 can only be successful if the mission is kept secret. That's the secret of its success. The missions undertaken are usually one-sided and self-serving, unorthodox and often questionable. It is rumoured that Double07 is licensed to kill without accountability. International policies and foreign diplomacies dictate an element of high secrecy to each mission. No effort is spared to keep all activities under the radar. National resources and all efforts are employed to support and to ensure the success of each mission.

We cannot operate likewise for our goal achieving. Why? Well, we are not Double07. We do not have the national talents and resources behind us to ensure our success. We need every public support and all encouragement to get on along the success path.

Declare and make public your goals. Do not keep them under cover. A declared goal would instill accountability and prevents pre-mature back out.

Step Six: Seek advice.

We all have our blind spots, with some are marginally obvious and the rest are completely oblivious. Besides, we developed specialised focuses and experiences that prevent us from seeing beyond our trained fields. To see beyond these limitations, one could read widely or pursue education outside one's domain. Or, you could seek advice and solicit input from someone with those expertise and experiences. Invaluable feedback and advice could prevent one from failing and help to stay on course.

In this chapter, we discussed some common possible obstacles to achieving our goals, and suggested ways to overcoming them. We shall put these learnings into practice by developing an Action Plan in the next chapter.

Chapter 6

Putting Them Together

Achieving goal could not stop at the discussion stage and concludes with a submission paper. This is not an academic exercise. Any worthy goal should not be left to chances. Action Plan has to be developed to pursue worthy goals and to follow through till their attainments. The end result should be an actual fulfillment of desired goals, a realisation of worthy dreams, and an improvement in personal effectiveness.

Yes, developing and executing an Action Plan is not a walk in the park, neither is it rocket science. It can be accomplished with relevant tools and knowledge. In this chapter we shall learn how to put together some of the tools we have discussed so far to develop an actionable plan.

Personal Effectiveness Action Plan

It's time to get the learnings from Part One and Part Two into action, and develop My Action Plan!

Referring to the familiar picture below, let's determine your goal (destination point B), identify your current situations (starting point A), and chart the effective course to achieve your goals (the Action Plan.)

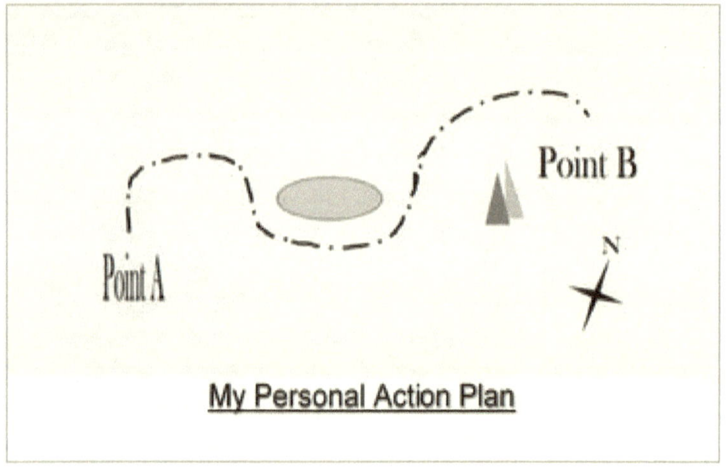

There are some simple steps and tools to help develop an actionable plan. The tools discussed so far would come in handy. Let's refer to the next table for the planning steps to develop an Action Plan.

The column on the left suggests the planning steps. The column on the right suggests suitable planning tools. One planning tool may be able to cover a few steps.

For example, the SMART goals planning tool may be suitable to define and prioritize the goals, and help to set deadlines too. These steps help to identify your worthy goals, your destination Point B.

Use a SWOT analysis planning tool to determine your strengths, weaknesses, opportunities and threats. These steps help to determine your current situation, your starting Point A.

Steps to Planning My Action Plan	Planning Tools
Define goals	SMART goals
Prioritize goals	
Set deadline	
Analyse strengths and weaknesses	SWOT analysis
Identify opportunities and threats	
Develop new skills	SOAR analysis
Define actions	
Seek support and feedback	
Chart progress and monitor achievement	Gantt chart

Use SOAR analysis to determine your strengths, opportunities, aspirations and results. This analysis may help identify what are some new skills that you need to pick up to enable you to achieve your goals.

When all these are done, seek feedback from some people whose opinions and advice you treasure. With these inputs, adjust your plan if need be. When the goals and activities are finalised, plot them onto a Gantt chart for project management. And you are ready to go!

After all these planning are done and your Action Plan is ready for execution, do be aware that this final plan is never really final. During the execution phase, it is likely issues and situations will surface that require change and adjustment to the original plan. Environmental factors may change, new technologies may surface, and new resources may become available. It is necessary to constantly monitor for any changes no matter how 'perfect' your original plan was. These changes can have direct and indirect impact on your original plan. Just do the necessary re-alignment and readjustment accordingly. And get going!

Develop My Growth Plan

Okay enough reading and discussion. Now is the time to get into action! Get some paper and a pen ready. Begin your Up My Personal Effectiveness by developing your Action Plan. Some helpful templates can be found in Appendix A. Let's get your Action Plan done before you proceed to the next chapter.

PART THREE

Manage Self Effectively

HONE ESSENTIAL SKILL-SETS

We are great at making impressive goals, or at least some kind of a wish list. Then we are equally great at procrastinating them. We are also pretty good at writing to-do-list. Then we are also pretty good at not following through the list. Resolutions made at the beginning of the year are meant to be broken at the end of the same year. Goals, plans and resolutions are meant to be made, not to be carried out. What is amazing is that this happened year after year, projects after projects! Their constancies are comparable to that of taxes and deaths. Why is this so?

A simple answer could be motivation, or rather a lack of it. However this phenomenon is more complex and deep-rooted to be explained by a single word. It deserves a closer examination. There are more than one factors and they can be intertwined. In the spirit of Up My Personal Effectiveness we shall attempt to break its code.

So why do we usually started off enthusiastically and energetically, but often end up deflated and defeated? Let's see how we can take step to break this cyclical curse of non-fulfillment. First, we set worthy and exciting goals. Goals provide directions, help focus and channel resources. Goals also clarify purposes and help determine if any essential skills and necessary tools should be acquired. The essential skills to manage self effectively would include time management, stress management and how to motivate self.

It is the aim of this Part Three Manage Self Effectively: Hone Essential Skill-Sets, to help you bridge the planning stage to actual doing, and beginning to realise dreams and accomplish goals. While the journey to managing self effectively can be uncertain, the skills and tools covered here are certainly a good start.

May your great journey to Up My Personal Effectiveness continues!

Chapter 7

Time Management and Organisation Skills

Really, time management? Time management is a misnomer. How can anyone manage time? Time is independent, not of any persuasion and totally merciless. It does not respect person nor status, power nor authority, and has a mind of its own. Time does not wait for anyone nor anything. It does not cooperate with you nor can it be tamed. So can you really manage time?

Why is there then such a big fuss about time management? There are huge number of books written on it, many expensive courses and workshops on how to help you manage your time. And we are talking about it here too? Well I suppose we are really talking about organising and managing activities, and time is the unit used to apportion the period for each activity. So this term is coined to refer to the organising and monitoring of tasks. And since this book is not a call for revolution, nor is its intention to cause any confusion, we shall continue to use this commonly used term for such a purpose.

So, time management shall stay as such in this discussion, though we really mean activity organisation and management. We shall use the term time management in this context.

Time is not equal

Each one of us is given the same exact amount of time each day, not a second more than another person. In this absolute term time is equal, fair, impersonal and impartial. However time is usually experienced in relative.

There are certain situations where time seems to move more quickly, and other situations where time seem to craw to a stand-still. For example when one is trying to flag a taxi in a rush to attend an appointment. With the left foot tapping double pace on the footpath, and the right index finger tapping uncontrollably on the watch, time seems to fly by very quickly. And no taxi seems to appear on any horizon! Every second seemed to tick by much more quickly than usual. Take another example when one is accidentally locked up in a chiller room awaiting for rescue. Every second seemed to tick by very slowly as the sub-zero temperature begins to work its magic on the mind while the body begins to freeze up. During this situation, time seems to snail and creep by very slowly. In these two examples, time was equal in absolute term but experienced in relative term. The perception of time is dependent on the situation, tends to be personal and therefore essentially relative.

Now a quick check on your perception on time relativity. Does time go by faster or slower at each of these situations: when you are with your boyfriend and when you are with your mother-in-law?

Yet some people seem to have more time to do all the things he wants, while the others seem to be running short of time most of the time doing the few things that he does not really want to. Is this also a perception of time at play? Well not exactly. These are more an issue of activity management. Okay, this is a Time Management issue, just to stay consistent with the term usage. Good time management skills could help one to be in control of one's activities and tasks, be more efficient and effective in accomplishing them, and provide a sense of direction and purpose.

What is Time Management

Time management refers to managing time effectively by allocating the right amount of time for the right activity at the right moment. To do this well one would need to be able to distinguish the important from the urgent activities, setting goals, learning to prioritise activities and delegating responsibilities. It involves effective planning, recognising time stealers and how to overcome them, and stop procrastination.

One of the most common challenges to time management is activity prioritisation. Spending too much time on something that is not critical nor important, leaving little time to do what is really important, often ending up in crises. So this person ends up with one crisis management after another, ending stressed up and irritable most of the time.

An effective way to prioritise activities and tasks is by separating the important from the urgent ones. Time Management Matrix can be helpful here.

Time Management Matrix

Time Management Matrix is a simple and useful tool to help us separate the important tasks from the urgent ones. Doing that helps us to prioritise our list of activities, and organise our Action Plan.

Let us first distinguish what is an important task and what is an urgent one. Important activities or tasks are those that will have a direct effect on your identified goals. Your goals will be jeopardised or compromised if these tasks are not duly completed. They are the "must-do" activities or tasks. For example if you plan to complete your first marathon. Gets into jogging and training the first 10 km will be important to your completing the full marathon.

Urgent activities or tasks are those that require immediate attention. Not dealing with these might have immediate consequences. To continue with the example above on your first marathon attempt. Reading and following the tweets and Instagram of your best friend's best friend on her ranting and complaining about her neighbour's cat is not going to help you complete your marathon. But they kept beeping and demanding your immediate attention.

A matrix of important and urgent results in 4 characteristics of activities or tasks. Let's take a look at the Time Management Matrix.

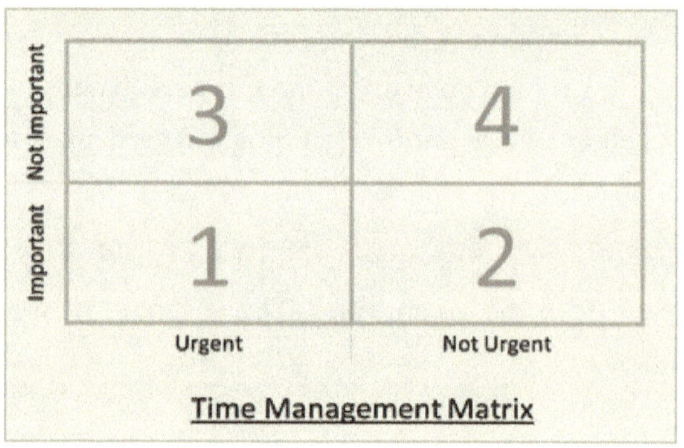

On the horizontal axis is the urgency scale. The vertical axis shows the importance scale. Simplified sectoring put the matrix into four quadrants. We shall label them as quadrant 1, 2, 3 and 4 as shown in the diagram above. Each quadrant shows distinct characteristics of activity.

Quadrant 1

This quadrant describes situations where activities are important with high urgency.

- These activities have direct effect on your identified goals
- They require immediate attention
- They are of high priority

This may be a crisis where one or some important tasks must be completed or addressed immediately to avoid any disastrous consequences or total failure of the desired goal. Not a comfortable situation to be in and should be reduced to the minimum possible if not be avoided totally. An example is your annual financial report to be submitted to the HQ office by tomorrow, and the Beijing and Tokyo offices have yet to submit their figures! You are not likely to have a good night, and would probably be doing some nasty things.

Quadrant 2

This quadrant describes situations where activities are important with low urgency.

- These activities have direct effect on your identified goals
- They do not need immediate attention
- They are for long term strategic planning

This is a desirable situation where important tasks or activities to accomplish a goal have been identified with ample or sufficient time to complete them. One has the benefit of time to consider, plan and execute the task. It can be an enjoyable process. We should aim to have most tasks in this ideal quadrant. An example is designing for your company next product range to be launched next year. This is only the beginning of the year and your assembled team is well ahead of the designing stages.

A note of caution: be conscientious in carrying out the required tasks according to plan and be careful to monitor their progress. Often these comfortable situations can deceive one to procrastinate tasks to quadrant 1.

Quadrant 3

This quadrant describes situations where activities are not important but with high urgency.

- These activities have no or little effect on your identified goals
- They demand immediate attention
- They can be minimised or delegated to others

These can be some deceptive or disruptive tasks that demand one's immediate attention and have no impact on your goals. Examples are phone calls or text messages. When a phone rings it shouts for your immediate attention, but usually has no relation to your current task. Learn to manage these tasks to prevent unnecessary distractions from your important goals. For example delegate the phone answering to another person.

Quadrant 4

This is a situation where the activities are not important and with low urgency.

- These activities have no or little effect on your identified goals
- They do not require immediate attention
- They are time wasters to be eliminated

These may appear to be neutral activities that would cause no harm to nobody. They float by you inconspicuously and then occupy your space and time. Examples are watching TV or playing computer games. These are time wasters and should be avoided at all costs. Or they will cost you dearly.

Consider your current activities. Which quadrant will you fit most of your daily activities onto? Do you have too many of them in quadrant 4? Do you have enough of them in quadrant 1 and 2?

Time Usage Analysis

One simple and effective way to analyse a person's current activities and priorities is to complete the Time Usage Analysis. This analysis provides a grand overview of your major and minor activities and occupations at a glance. The analysis chart looks like a typical one week time table. 7 columns representing the 7 days of the week and 3 rows dividing each day into morning, noon and evening.

Time Usage Analysis

sun	mon	tue	wed	thu	fri	sat

Simple steps to complete your Time Usage Analysis.

- Record the typical activities that occupy each day, separating the morning, noon and evening

- Use hourly block to be effective. Go down to half-hourly if need be

- Use different colour or shading for similar activities. This provides further clarity

- Once completed, you will be able to see which/what are your main occupations and priorities

Time Usage Analysis (Illustration only)						
sun	mon	tue	wed	thu	fri	sat
Volunteer work	Office, work					Exercise time
Social	Family time					

The illustrated example of a Time Usage Analysis above provides a quick view of what activities occupy a normal week. We can see that work occupies most of the days in a typical week, leaving the evenings for family time, and the weekends for volunteer work and relaxation. Re-organisation and adjustment can be made if these activities do not sit well with the indented life's priorities. For example if we see the whole Time Usage Analysis occupied by work only for all the 7 days, it should scream loud that immediate and urgent action must be taken to the weekly activities. What needs to be done would depend very much on the desired life's goals. For example if this person desires more family time, then he would need to get back home early some of the days, and intentionally reserve one of the weekends for family time.

Challenges and Responses to Effective Time Management

No road can run a straight course indefinitely. It has to curve to bend around a building, a hill or a water body. Even on a flat desert terrain where a road can be expected to run a straight course for miles on, a driver may encounter some loose sand surfaces, or some dead animals on it. These present challenges to the driver and require appropriate responses.

Similarly, effective time management is likely to meet challenges as well. Challenges come in different formats and fashions. Some of them are easier to deal with while others need more effort. We shall discuss some common barriers and their appropriate corresponding responses to effective time management.

Lack of clear goals or direction

A very common challenge to effective time management is a lack of clear goal or direction. If a ship sails in the open sea without a destination, it will merely be drifted by the wind and tossed by the wave. Without a clearly defined destination, the ship has not made any progress even if it has traveled for miles and days.

Similarly without a clearly defined goal, one is not able to start the journey. He knows not what resources to mobilise nor which plan to execute. There can be no activity to start for none will make sense. Thus there is no need to manage time.

Some simple steps to overcome this challenge:

- Set goals
- Determine the current situation
- Draw out an Action Plan

Please refer to Part Two of this book for detailed steps to goal setting and developing an action plan.

Inability to say no

Everyone wants to be nice, even if being nice could mean a little inconvenience to oneself in some other ways. There are times we are expected, or demanded to be interrupted to fulfill some other people's interests. They can be your seniors, superiors or bosses. Their requests become part of our tasks that usually have no effect or rather, could have a direct conflict to our desired goals. Whether due to our position or personality, we are unable to say no to them. Unable to separate the important tasks from those not important ones does not help either. Inability to say no to such requests can derail our own activity management.

One way to overcome such challenges is to first have clear goals and an action plan. Get these done by following the earlier discussions. When these are done important activities and tasks would become very clear, thereby help us to identify those not important ones. When you have sifted the important tasks through, we can then learn to delegate or say no to the not important ones.

Put these responses into step as follow:

- Set goals and draw out an action plan
- Determine the important activities, and identify the not important ones
- Commit to achieving the goals
- Learn to delegate
- Learn to say "no"

Time wasters or time stealers

Time wasters or time stealers are activities or tasks that are not important nor urgent to your desired goals. They can be a movie that you want to watch or a newly loaded computer game that you want to play. Our lethargy is their lethality. They appear as some innocent little activities that are supposed to provide some relaxation time. Then little but surely they would take your time and attention away from your important tasks.

Follow these simple steps to arrest time-waster:

- Time wasters are the not important not urgent activities
- Use Time Management Matrix to list out time-wasters, those

in quadrant 4

- Avoid time wasters, or they will shift your quadrant 2 into quadrant 1

Negative Attitude/mind-set

Negative attitude does not make a grand entry. No one likes to have it nor intentionally plans to acquire it. It usually creeps in unannounced. By the time one is aware of its presence, great harm awaits, if not already descended. While it is shy in arrival, it is not so in refusal to leave.

Negative attitude or mind-set could have developed due to low self-worth or low self-esteem. A negative environment where affirmation and positive reinforcement are lacking could be responsible for this low esteem. Negative attitude could have developed due to many past failures and unsatisfactory attempts too. There is no desire to manage activity if one expects only negative outcomes or failures. Just leave them to luck or chance. And this attitude becomes a self-fulfilling prophecy.

Take the following steps to overcome a negative attitude:

- Reaffirm the worthiness of goals that one is trying to achieve
- Remind oneself of previous successes
- Work out a reward system to motivate positive actions
- Ask for help from friends and family members.

Lack of Motivation

A close cousin of negative attitude, motivation lacking usually follows. They seem like a pair of inseparable twins. It works to the same exploits if not greater than a negative attitude. Together they delay decision making and hamper execution, pushing important activities from urgency to crisis and onto redundancy. Inactivity becomes the norm, non-accomplishment the status.

Get into the following steps to get out of low motivation:

- Set worthy goals that are personal and relatable. State them in tangible terms
- Break down long term goals into realistic short term goals. Adjust and re-align them when necessary
- Reward yourself when you hit the short term goals
- Find something to motivate you, consider the pain and pleasure options

More details on self-motivation will be covered in Chapter 9.

Procrastination

Every one of us is guilty of this. It is only human. Our brains choose auto-pilot mode for repeated chores to avoid thinking and to conserve energy. We are designed for preservation to take the path of least resistance. We will delay difficult tasks and avoid challenging activities if possible. We will only do them if we really have to, and if possible do them later.

So you see, to procrastinate is human. And we must see further than our humanity: this part of human nature can harm us. Big time! Procrastination has the same potential as the above pair of twins to push our important tasks from urgency to crisis and onto complete disaster.

The following steps could help address procrastination:

- Break the task into smaller manageable chunks
- Begin with easy tasks to build momentum
- Reward yourself when you accomplished each task
- Set a deadline and stick to it

Technologies and methods to manage time

There are many good tools around to help us manage time efficiently. They are not costly and you can DIY if you fancy. Some of these are "To-do list", "Post-it notes" reminder, "Weekly schedule planner" and our plain old Time-table. You can easily find royalty-free ones and download them from the net as well.

There are apps and computer versions for those who prefer to work on electronic devices. One advantage of these is that they can be linked up onto various platforms and devices, besides allowing real time changes and updates. These features can be really neat. Examples are "Google Business Calendar", "EssentialPIM", and "WinCalendar". Handphone apps for electronic calendar, schedule planner, note pad are available. A drawback with these devices and apps is that they can become a distraction. So instead of manage time, we need to manage these devices as well.

You can check this link for a list of time management tools.

https://www.scoro.com/blog/best-time-management-tools-reviewed/

Chapter 8

Stress Management Skills

Stress is not necessarily bad. It was stress that kept us away from dangerous animals of the wild in the past, which helped us stayed alive. With a healthy dose, stress can help us perform under pressure and deliver our best. However as with any other overdoses, it can harm our body and mind, relationships and everything we do. We will discuss the latter type of stress in this chapter. It is essential to learn to recognise the signs and symptoms of overdosed stress, and take steps to reduce, if not remove its harmful effects.

Recognise Symptoms and Signs of Stress and Ways to Manage Stress Effectively

What is Stress? Stress is a state of mental or emotional strain or tension resulting from adverse or demanding circumstances. It is our body's way of responding to any of these stimuli. When one senses danger, whether real or imagined, the body natural response kicks in. This automatic process is known as the "fight-or-flight" reaction or the "stress response".

The stress response is the body's way of protecting oneself. It helps one stay focus and alert. In extreme cases stress can save life. For example in the face of imminent danger of a fast-approaching car, stress gives one the extra energy to dash off and jump away into safety.

Stress can be helpful in many occasions. It helps one keep focus during a game. It helps one to concentrate during an examination. It helps one stay focus when preparing for an important presentation tomorrow. However going beyond a certain point, stress starts to cause damages to one's mind and body, affecting productivity and quality of life. Some effects of chronic stress could be depression and anxiety, pain of any kind, digestive problems and heart disease.

Causes of Stress

Causes of stress are like the sharp needle at close proximity to an over-inflated balloon. The balloon being likened to an existing stress. Any further inflation of the balloon or an inching of the needle toward the balloon and the explosion would result. Usually with embarrassing outcomes at best or devastating ones at worst. Learn to recognise the needle that could burst the balloon and remove it well before they get too close to each other. That could help defuse tense situations.

Causes of stress can come from two factors: the internal and the external. Internal factors are usually self-generated. Examples when one worries excessively about a certain event that may or may not occur, or just an inexplicable pessimism about life. External factors are easier to identify. It could be a coming major examination, an important presentation, or a heavy work schedule.

Some Common Internal Causes of Stress

- Pessimism
- Not accepting uncertainty
- Negative self-talk
- Unrealistic expectations
- Perfectionism
- Un-forgiveness

Some Common External Causes of Stress

- Major life changes, like marriage
- Work or school load
- Unstable relationship
- Financial problems
- Family issues
- Illnesses

Symptoms and Signs of Stress

Symptoms and signs of stress can be manifested in various forms. They may not show clearly and usually creep up unannounced along with time. They can be difficult to detect. One may even get used to them and dismiss them as inconsequential. It is therefore important to be aware of the common symptoms and signs of overdosed stresses. Symptoms and signs of stress can come in any or combination of the four forms: physical, cognitive, emotional and behavioural.

Physical Symptoms

- Aches and pains
- Upset stomach
- Nausea, dizziness

- Chest pain, racing heart
- Difficulty sleeping
- Clenched jaws
- Grinding teeth
- Shoulder and back pain

Thinking Based Symptoms

- Memory problems
- Unable to concentrate
- Constant worrying
- Negative thinking
- Difficulty in learning
- Unable to make decision
- Loss sense of humour
- Lack of creativity

Emotional Symptoms

- Depression
- Anxiety and agitation
- Irritability and anger
- Feeling loneliness
- Frequent mood swings
- Nervousness
- Sadness
- Feeling powerless

Behavioural Symptoms

- Eating more or eating less
- Sleeping too much or too little
- Withdrawal from social situations
- Drug abuse, alcohol
- Procrastination
- Bossiness
- Explosive actions
- Critical attitude of others

These symptoms may be indicative but not conclusive. Do not be too quick to self-diagnose and declare yourself a stress victim if you notice some of these symptoms. They can be due to other causes as well. Consult the doctor if in doubt. Meantime please do not get yourself unduly stressed over stresses.

Techniques/tools to manage stress

There are techniques and tools to help manage stress. These are good recommendations to follow even after the doctor had declared you a non-stressed victim, and great suggestions if you still suspect yourself to be one. Some guidelines and approaches to manage stress would be to:

Kick those stress-causing habits

Some habits are not helpful in life generally and for time management in particular. Habits like procrastinating and over-reacting could get one into stressful situations. Recognise them early and address them accordingly would be helpful. Look at Chapter 7 on how to handle procrastination. Over-reacting is addressed in the next point.

Replace over-reactive behaviours with reasonable ones

Overacting often arose due to unclear, partial or wrong facts. These lead to wrong interpretation of situations and cause undue stresses. For example one can misread a shorter deadline of a project than actual, or misinterprets a sender's message as negative. These could cause the receiver of the information to over-react into panic or fall into a rage.

Jump not into conclusion based on incomplete or first data. First get the complete data. Then seek clarification from the correct source to form an accurate and complete assessment of the situation. It would then be a suitable time to respond accordingly.

Learn to stay calm

The ability to stay calm and level-headed is helpful to handle stressful situations. Try to detach emotion from the issue at hand. This helps one not to overreact and puts one's temper under check. Sure, these are easier said than done, simpler to preach than to practise. But with determination and practice, it is achievable. One tested way to stay calm is simply to count up to 10 before reacting. Try it. It works!

Take ownership

One quick test before we proceed on. Did you just count to 10? No? Right, now you know if you have learnt to stay calm.

Take ownership of one's emotions and reactions. Over-reacting and blowing off temper would occur frequently and repeatedly when one does not take ownership of these behaviours. Take ownership means to salvage the situations, to recover the damages, to apologise to the people involved and to pay for all penalties that your uncontrolled reaction caused. No excuses, no discount. Make full restitution to all damages. Behaviour would change when one begins to take responsibility for the outcomes of these habits. The motivation to change before you next blow your top would be much stronger when you have learnt to take ownership of your own emotions.

Ask help from friends and family members

If all of the above fails, seek help from friends and family members. One may not be able to think clearly nor consider suitable options when under a stressful situation. Acting as a non-involved third party, they may offer untainted perspectives, providing suggestions and recommendations that could be helpful. Be willing to listen to their inputs and ready to accept their offers to help.

Helpful Habits against Stress

You can improve your ability to handle stress by:

Get into physical moment

Increase physical activities can help relieve stress. Regular exercises can relieve one from stress points and also help lift one's mood. They break the cycle of negative thoughts and allow one to think positively. Physical activities like walking, jogging, swimming and rhythmic dancing could be effective. These activities can be done by oneself. Get someone along if that helps. Just get moving, then continue doing!

Connecting with others

Meeting people, connecting with friends and talking to family members could help relieve stress and make one feel better. We are social beings, and we will do well by connecting to another being. A brief exchange of kind words or a simple message of concern with another human being helps one feel good and being appreciated. Spend time connecting with people and building meaningful relationships. Technologies are making this connecting much easier. You can WhatsApp, Skype and Zoom anytime, anywhere at no cost. The secret of success to this strategy is to start connecting with people, don't wait for them to get to you.

Engage your senses

Engaged senses can help relieve stress. Senses include sight, sound, taste, smell or touch. Listening to inspiring songs, smelling the flowers, or petting an animal can be helpful. Different people respond to different levels for different senses. One would need to find out which senses work well for oneself. The secret to success for this strategy? Yes, get going!

Eat a healthy diet

Diet can affect one's mood and by extension one's handling of stress. Eating a diet full of processed and convenience food, refined carbohydrates, and sugary snacks can worsen symptoms of stress. A diet rich in fresh fruits and vegetables, omega-3 fatty acids and high-quality protein, can help one better cope with stress. These are general guides, I am not a trained dietician. Nor am I advertising for or against any diet. But this is generally helpful for your healthy eating if it does nothing to help reduce stress.

So, eating right, exercising enough, resting well, engaging the senses and connecting with people can keep one stress-free or less stressful. All these suggestions are not that stressful to follow, is it? And finally, smile more often!

Chapter 9

Self-Motivation Skills

It is easy to mistaken Eng for Seng, and vice versa. Well they are identical twins. However when you begin a conversation with them, the differences become evident. Eng has this what-ever-will-be-will-be attitude toward work and everything else in life. Nothing is worth striving for nor working hard toward. Everything has been as it has always been, and will continue to be. You cannot really affect any change: tomorrow will be just like yesterday, no matter what you do today.

Seng the elder twin is pretty much the opposite. He is energetic and positive toward the tasks he wants to accomplish. He strives hard and seeks higher goals after each success. Seng likes to effect change, and tomorrow is going to be better than today. It is not difficult to see why more people like to hang out with Seng and avoid Eng if possible. While this motivates Seng further, it does not bother Eng any bit at all.

While Eng and Seng may look alike, apparently their futures would be anything but alike. Their differing motivation, which is related to their personal values and perspective in life, directs that their future would unlikely coincide.

Most of us would probably not look like another person unless you have an identical twin too. However each of us can probably be placed into one of these 2 groups. Some of us are more "Engese", while some are more "Sengese". And the rest can fall somewhere in-between.

Motivation

We will take a closer look at the motivation that distinguishes Eng from Seng. Self-motivation in particular. Motivation refers to the needs, desires, wants or drives within an individual. It involves getting people to act and to accomplish the desired goals.

There are two main types of motivators, the intrinsic and the extrinsic.

Intrinsic, or sometimes known as internal motivators are those to do with motives that come from within a person. The tasks or goals are related to those that one wants to do, and the sense of accomplishment comes from a job well done. Some of the intrinsic motivators are having fun, being interested and personal challenge.

Extrinsic, or sometimes known as external motivators are those that come from outside a person. The tasks or goals are related to those that one has to do. There is a sense of obligation and having to do them because someone else wants us to. Or they are done to obtain some kind of external rewards like money, power and good marks or grades.

Either type of motivator can be good enough to get difficult tasks done, while that of intrinsic would perceive to be more desirable and enjoyable. However, it is not uncommon that both of them work together for greater effect. Different people are motivated differently, and at different stages of life, their sources of motivation may differ. A similar task could be differently motivated for different people. Okay, all these differing differences are getting pretty confusing. Suffice to say that a self-motivated person would enjoy accomplishing tasks and completing goals. So, let's join the Seng tribe!

Self-Motivation

A person can be motivated by internal or external factors or a combination of both. Self-motivation in its simplest form is what drives a person to complete tasks. The internal motivators are very high. Self-motivation is an essential skill to up my personal effectiveness. It is the ability to do whatever needed to be done by oneself without any external influence. A self- motivated person is able to carry through and complete tasks with satisfactory outcomes. He is able to find a reason to complete even those challenging tasks without needing someone else to encourage or push him on.

Elements of motivation

Let us now look at the elements of motivation to helps improve self-motivation.

Personal drive

Personal drive refers to the desire to achieve and to accomplish goals. It could be seen as aggressive ambitions, the positive ones.

Persons with high drive are those with a growth mentality. They believe their abilities and capabilities can grow to accomplish greater things. They are ready to work harder and keen to improve their skills. Their outlook is positive and they exhibit high energy. They are the Seng tribe.

People who lack personal drive are those with a fixed mentality. They believe talent is 'gifted' - if you have it, you have it. If you don't have it, well you don't. There is nothing you can do to improve the lots. As such there is no reason to work any harder. They are the Eng tribe.

Commitment to goals

Goal setting gets worthy goals to be identified, and can certainly help one to be more effective. Goal provides a focal point and helps one to stay committed. Commitment to goals is the ability to stay on the course, and the willingness to do all the activities to accomplish the goals, regardless if they are enjoyable or not. A kind of 'bite-the-bullet' stubborn attitude to follow through until the goal is reached.

Initiative

Initiative is the readiness and willingness to act on opportunities. This has to be distinguished from foolishness and speculation, where one jumps blindly onto anything that moves.

Good initiative takes into account all relevant factors and take sufficient time to consider before making a decision. In situations where not all information is available, it has the courage to take a calculated risk. It is a combination of courage and willingness to take good risks.

Resilience and optimism

Resilience is the ability to keep on going on to pursue goals in the face of continuous setbacks. One just gets up when he falls, bounces back after each setback.

Optimism is the ability to always look on the bright side, to see possibility in unfavourable situations. It allows one to be creative and think out of the box for solutions.

Resilience and optimism usually work together to stay through and work out solutions in difficult situations.

Get Motivated

You would be enjoying life and achieving goals at the same time if you managed to get into the Seng tribe. Congratulation! You tend to work better and love what you are doing. You'll find it easier to spring out of bed early in the morning, and are excited at work, and be happy in general.

Do not despair if you find yourself in the Eng tribe. There are ways and helps to get motivated and enjoy life along the way. Try the following for they can positively help you get motivated.

Let's Get Motivated!

Get positive

It's pretty hard to get anything done if we stay in the Eng tribe with a fixed mentality. We will find it difficult to crawl out of bed and get excited each morning when we see no prospect of gaining success or improvement to a situation. No one could begin to experience success if no action is taken at all! This is a self-fulfilling downward spiral ending.

When negative thoughts begin to fester, recognise that you have the power to say 'stop' to that. Refocus on the tasks at hand, work out a strategy and action plan to accomplish them. All tasks can be accomplished, all challenges can be overcome. Acquire new skills or learn new tools if need be. Besides, you can always ask for help, perhaps from the Seng tribe. Reframe the situation in a positive way. This is not about thinking positively (and does nothing else). It is about getting positive, getting into actions that will contribute toward the desired goals. If necessary, this may be time to kick your butt, really hard.

Get confident

Once you are in the Seng tribe and acquired the growth mentality, begin to work on your confidence.

Recollect and recall your past successes. List them down, in detail if possible, no matter what they were and how small they appeared to you. What did you do, with what resources, any challenges and how you overcame them. These artifacts form your portfolio of successes, testimonies that you have the capacity and ability to get things done!

Get hungry

Well, we are not talking about the hunger that can be satisfied with pizza or pie. This hunger refers to a deep or desperate desire to want to achieve the identified goal. It is unlike looking at another piece of fried chicken wing sitting on the plate right in front of you just after completing a 10-course dinner. The desire to eat that piece of fried chicken wing will be lacking if not repulsive. This same piece of chicken wing will have a different appeal if you have been fasting for the last 24 hours. Very often those who are not motivated are still digesting their 10-course dinner.

Linking a difficult task that is beginning to get draggy to another goal can be helpful. For example, you want to go on a holiday. Tie the completion of writing the project proposal to going for that holiday. That could get you hungry to complete the proposal.

Set large goals

Set goals that are big and would 'hunger' you. Small goals or those that you have achieved many times over easily become mundane and routine chores. For example you have been jogging a mile 3 times a week for the last 3 years, or swimming 10 laps 10 times a month for the last 10 years. These would not excite nor motivate you.

Set for yourself excitable and large goals, and step up to greater challenges and motivating goals. Maybe attempt the 4-minutes mile or the triathlon? What could be your large excitable goal?

Keep it small

This is not a contradiction to the previous point. This is a proven strategy to accomplish big goals. Hear me out.

How do you eat an elephant? If you really want to do that, well do that one bite at a time.

Any lofty goal may appear impossible to achieve at first glance. Remember Rome was not built in one day and the Great Wall of China took many years to complete too. Break down your goal into smaller manageable tasks and accomplish them. One at a time.

Every wonderful journey began with the first step. Then the next. And the next. Until you reach the end of the rainbow. This is a great strategy to accomplish a large goal by breaking it into smaller ones.

Track your progress

Tracking progresses provides a sense of accomplishment and success. It gives a sense of purpose and direction. Signs of Progress indicate positive outcomes and generate the drive to continue. It is critically essential and simply motivating. Never lose sight of where you are, and you will not lose sight of where you have been. Then you will know where you must be going.

Celebrate

Celebrates every accomplishment and rewards each success regardless if they are big or small ones. Celebrations help track and mark progress. They are largely contagious and motivating. Celebrations need not be huge budget. A small break to announce achievement, or a 5-minutes hi-five session to mark milestone can be elevating.

Know setbacks will happen

Setbacks and failures are processes, they are not deterministic nor final. Recognise that setbacks and failures will happen. Only simple routine tasks do not expect setbacks. That's why they are called chores. Setbacks are part of the package for grand challenging goals.

Be careful especially if you are a perfectionist. Setbacks and failures have nothing to do with you. Nor are they any indication of your ability or capability. Yes, they may happen due to your planning neglects or approach errors, but they can happen simply because of situations or factors that are beyond anyone's control as well. You are not necessarily responsible for them.

Regardless, just get up right back sooner. Reassess the situation, readjust and realign if need be. Then get on getting on.

Get into Seng tribe

Seriously, people around us do affect and influence us. The right group of people can expand our horizons and motivate us to greater heights. The reverse is equally true. Negative people will narrow our outlook and limit our growth. It is important that we get into and surround ourselves with people of growth mentality. Seek out people with the values and qualities that would help you become a better achiever. They would welcome and accept anyone who genuinely seeks to improve oneself.

Let's get into the Seng tribe!

PART FOUR

Work with Others

Hone Overcoming Skill-Sets

Human are not individuals living on an island all by oneself. We band together with other individuals in communities and thrive as tribes, though some modern cultures may try to persuade us that we can do otherwise.

Humans are motivated by survival instinct and essentially self-serving. It is not easy for humans to live together and get along for an extended period of time. It is a near miracle that we made it so far and become so successful. We are successful because we have developed overcoming skills. These skills allow us to work effectively as teams, and to live harmoniously as communities. These are factors that not only allow us to survive thus far, but also overcome overwhelming odds against animals which are physically much stronger and faster than us, and against environments that are harsh and sometimes uninhabitable to us. These do not come naturally – they are learnt skills, probably after much tragedy and death.

Effective communication allows us to share thoughts and ideas, organising ourselves into effective teams, and achieving tasks that are much greater than any single individual could accomplish. Working as a team was critical for our survival and successes, and will continue to be so. Communication is an essential overcoming skill for us to work effectively as a team.

Sure, we have learnt to work as a team and live as a community, we are nevertheless comprised of individuals. An individual has its unique personality, preference and perspective. Differences and diversities surface when individuals come together. Disagreements, discomforts and conflicts converge to clashes when we try to live together. Conflict resolution skill allows us to put aside our individualities, work out our differences and live amicably as communities.

To stay successful and on top of this game, we need to learn to live and work with others by honing overcoming skill-sets.

Chapter 10

Communicate Effectively to Bridge Diversity

We do this all day, all the while! Are we not communicating when we talk to one another? Well, there is more to communication than just talking to another person.

We take communication pretty much for granted assuming it is the same as talking. But talking is not, neither is speaking, communication. Talking can be done by oneself, so can speaking be. And though we have been doing that since we were babies, yet we are not very good at it. That is why we sometimes hear this comment: "Listen to what you are talking about!" This is a rude feedback that you are not talking sense, or you are not communicating effectively. Often the "listening" part is rather lacking in our communication.

For an example of how communication can be more than just words, let's consider this statement: "Can you hand over the broom?" Is this a question about your ability to do something, handing over the bloom, or is it a request for you to do something? Most people would assume the latter for this example, and they are probably right. But the question is equally valid for the former. It may not be that clear in other examples. The intended message may be different from the apparent texts.

Communication requires at least 2 parties: it involves one party sending a message and the other receiving it. Effective communication refers to the skill of transmitting your message in such a way that the other party receiving it can interpret your intended meaning accurately.

Effective communication is essential for most occasions and critical for specific situations. An example where effective communication is critical would be in a surgical room. It is critical that surgeons and the assisting nurses understand each other very well during surgery. The nurses must understand every instruction from the surgeons. The surgeon would ask for various tools during a surgical operation. Each tool is unique and specific for a particular task. The assisting nurses need to know exactly what is expected and hand over the exact tool each time. There is no room for error, no margin for mistake, any miscommunication could have devastating consequences.

Why is communication important

Humans need to communicate because we are social beings and we do not live on an island alone. Banding together as communities helps us survive thus far. The ability to communicate with one another helps us overpower wild animals stronger and faster than us, overcomes harsh uninhabitable environments, and thrives as communities. We built skyscrapers and sent man into outer space with complex communication systems. It is no exaggeration to say that humans would have no chance of surviving wild animals, less any of these achievements if not for our ability to communicate.

A simple illustration of how communication is important. Two men on a canoe are trying to cross over to the next bank of a fast-flowing river. The man with the paddle is blindfolded while the man without the paddle is not allowed to speak. The arrangement is for the first man to provide the propelling power while the second man to instruct direction and warning of any danger. It is not difficult to foresee that such a venture will end up in failure, if not disaster.

What is Communication

Communication happens between two parties; one party has an information to share and the other party receiving it. And there is a need for a mean or mode of transmitting this information. These 2 parties and the mode of transmission have to play their respective roles well for communication to take place. Any malfunction or non-function from any one of these will result in miscommunication or non-communication, which can hurt feelings, frustrates relationships and jeopardies cooperation.

For example a sender of the message says: "How are you?" The medium (maybe a phone) carrying the message is functioning well and no distortion occurs to the message. Then the receiver will receive a clear "How are you?" message, felt appreciated and responds accordingly. If however, the message was distorted and the word "are" was left out, then the receiver would hear the message as "How you" This statement appeared to be incomplete and the receiver will be expecting more data coming in. He would become very puzzled and perplexed when no further data were forthcoming. This is a case of miscommunication.

Types of communication

While it is true that communication is more than just speaking, it is equally true that it is commonly conducted through verbal means. Some other types of communication are non-verbal and written communication.

Verbal communication

This is the most common form of communication. We talk to one another daily. One party wants to transmit a piece of information, say it aloud to another person who receives the message, and a verbal communication occurred. It is also one of the most misunderstood forms and taken very much for granted. You assumed and took for granted that whatever you wanted to say would be received by the other party just as you meant it to be. However, if you are not careful, often the meaning was received with different interpretations. This can happen due to differing values, cultures, contexts, perspectives and a whole lot of possible emotional interpretations. A misunderstanding occurs due to these differences, a suspicion arises, and the argument begins, resulting in frustrations and hurt feelings.

You can improve your verbal communication and raise its effectiveness with the following tips:

Speak clearly

Speak loud enough for the other party to hear, and speak clearly without murmuring or "eating" your words so that the other party can receive your message without distortion or with any missing words, and understand you fully. Let it be audible.

Choose your word

Use appropriate words that suit the listener's level of understanding. Don't use office jargon in a social context, and vice versa. Be aware of cultural differences too, some words are not acceptable in another culture as compared to yours. Neither is choosing big, bombastic words always helpful in communicating. While you may be impressed by your eloquence, listeners may be depressed by your egoism.

Use appropriate tone

The tone, or the sound of your voice powerfully transmits your feeling. Choose an appropriate tone that matches the message to the feeling you are trying to express. It is not helpful using the tone suitable for a toddle to your key customer. Neither is it effective to raise 3-octave levels when communicating with co-workers.

Remember your audience

Adjust your communication style to suit your audience. You want to use a different style when speaking to a five year child and when you speak to your important customer. It is helpful to change your communication style when speaking to your husband and to your male colleague. This will avoid many unnecessary embarrassing situations.

Non-Verbal communication

Most people neglect or are ignorant of this non-verbal communication because, well, it is non-verbal! However studies and researches show that non-verbal communication is a very important part of communication. Some research suggests that up to 93% of communication is non-verbal. It will do you good to begin paying attention to this form of communication.

You communicate non-verbally through your facial expressions, postures and body language. Learning to understand and interpret these non-verbal cues would help you "hear" the major part of the message. This skill helps you confirm and ascertain the words you are hearing if they match the non-verbal, or if the person is paying attention to the conversation? Being aware of non-verbal communication would help you transmit your message better and effectively too. Be mindful that your non-verbal communication matches that of your verbal one.

Some of the following non-verbal cues can help improve your effectiveness.

Eye contact

Maintain good eye contact with your dialog partner. No, do not stare. Just look pleasantly at the eyes. This shows that you are interested in and are paying attention to the conversation. Looking away shows distraction or disinterest, and constantly looking down indicates shyness or lack of confidence.

Pace or speed of speech

Speaking at a pace that differs from that of your conversation partner may not be effective. Speaking too fast risks losing some words, and the message may be distorted. It also gives the impression that you are in a hurry or impatient. Speaking too slowly may risk losing your audience as he wandered off. Match your pace with your audience is a good guide.

Crossed arms or legs

The crossing of arms or legs can indicate rejection, disinterested or guarded. Be mindful of these hidden messages, unless these are what you want to send.

Posture or body position

The distance between you and your audience send out different messages. Standing too close causes discomfort, while standing too far put a distance. What is the appropriate distance depends on cultural acceptance and norms. Leaning body forward generally shows interest or sincerity, leaning away may indicate disgust or disapproval. Sure, watch your distance when leaning forward, showing too much interest can be inappropriate.

Facial Expressions

Putting on a wide smile while discussing an important subject would indicate your lack of seriousness and professionalism. Wearing a glum expression during a company D&D would raise wrong kind of attention. Your facial expression tells your personality and mood. It can draw people toward you or repels them. Be aware of what you are wearing on your face when you talk, not just the jewelry. Generally, it is good to wear a relaxed smile.

Written communication

Writing is another common form of communication. It was mainly used in formal occasions like government announcements or letters, official statements or official letters. But are getting common for personal and social contexts.

Written communication in social contexts is gaining popularity in the form of blogs, Facebook and twitters. Formal written communication sticks to the fact and accurate information, using proper grammar and punctuation, void of personal feeling or opinion. The language and style can be rather sterile. The intent is to get the fact across accurately. Social context tends to be more personable, with feeling words and sometimes colourful. The intent is to share happenings surrounding a person or object of interest. In either case, the choice of the written word needs to align with the intent and to ensure effective communication.

Active Listening

Listening is an important component of communication. While much attention is given to the transmitting party, the receiving party plays a critical role to complete the communication process. Indeed it takes two parties to make a clap. It was asserted that to be a good communicator one has to first learn to be a good listener.

There is a distinction between active listening to simply hearing. Active listening refers to the effort made to understand what the other party is trying to communicate; listening to the spoken words and observing the non-verbal cues. Active listening involves not just the ear, it also includes using the eyes to "hear" the unspoken messages. Effective communication involves all the functioning of the ear, the mouth and the eye, and a whole lot of other senses as well.

You can improve your listening skill with the following tips:

Give attention to the speaker

Focus on the speaker and make eye contact. When the mind wanders off, get it back to the conversation soonest. Avoid holding your smartphone in the hand during a conversation, never lift it up to swipe.

Try to understand

During those moments, despite your listening and you still don't understand what is been said, seek clarification by asking follow-up questions. Do not pretend that you understand when you don't.

Wait for your turn to speak

Do not interrupt when you have a point to make, wait for an appropriate break to make your clarification. When you demonstrate respect to the speaker, it will be reciprocated as well.

Show interest

Show interest in the conversation by making a little nod of the head. A simple small "yes" and "hmm" would encourage the speaker.

Rephrase

Repeat what was said in your own word allows you to clarify with the speaker and helps you better understand the message. Rephrasing a message helps you remember it better too.

Set aside judgment

Set aside your personal judgment and withhold blame, listen to the full message. This will help you understand the message.

Challenges to Effective Communication

There are many reasons for how communication could breakdown. The speaker not speaking well, the listener not hearing right or a bad choice of the transmission mode. Any non-functioning of the 3 components to communication could cause frustration. Active listening, seeking clarification and reflection could help reduce such incidences. Yet, there are some common barriers to effective communication.

Use of jargon

Jargons are technical terms or complicated trade lingos. They are developed over time within a trade or community to foster bonding and simplify communication. Jargons are however, unfamiliar if not alien to people outside the trade or community. These people could feel excluded and unwelcomed. Avoid using jargon especially when there are "outsiders" in the conversation.

Lack of focus

You can't communicate well when you multitask. Avoid distractions and stay focus to communicate well. Many traffic accidents could have been avoided if the drivers were not on the phone while at the wheel. Give your attention to the person in front of you, this is the least courtesy you should return for all her effort to get to you.

Inconsistent body language

Listener will get confused when you say something while your non-verbal indicates another thing else. For example saying you care to a 4-year-old child with your hands on the hips and a stern face convey conflicting messages. Let your non-verbal messages be consistent with your verbal ones.

Cultural differences

Social norms and mores differ in different cultures. Take for example the concept of personal space. Some cultures need a bigger personal space while others can tolerate a closer one. Another culture forbids padding on a child's head. The parents would reject you as impolite at best, or view your action as with ill intention at worst. Know the cultural difference to convey the correct message.

Expectations and prejudices

People often heard what they were expecting to hear rather than what is actually being said. Or they may interpret your message according to their prejudices. These end up with inaccurate conclusions.

Language differences

Difficulty in understanding unfamiliar accents or other foreign languages. These present a challenge to communication.

Effective Communication Skills

Effective communication is not just about information exchange. It is understanding the emotion and intention behind the message. The following skills could help in effective communication.

- Active listening
- Non-verbal communication
- Appropriate questioning techniques

We have just covered Active listening and non-verbal, we will next discuss questioning techniques that could help us communicate more effectively.

Appropriate Questioning Techniques

Appropriate questioning techniques are helpful skills to clarify information or arguments. These techniques when employed appropriately could defuse heated situations and clarify matters. These questioning techniques could help decipher and establish the core message. They help effective communicating. Let's look at some appropriate questioning techniques.

Open-ended question

Open-ended questions are those that allow further elaboration. Example "Could you tell me more about …?" Open-ended questions are useful when you want to request for more information or to seek more details.

Closed-ended question

Closed-ended questions seek to confirm a point. They usually anticipate a "Yes" or "No" response. Example "Did you come to town this week?" Closed-ended questions can be effective when you seek to establish facts or to confirm information.

Leading question

Leading questions prompt or encourage the answer wanted. Example "You have been involved in Project X since the beginning, right?" Leading questions help to confirm certain information. They can also be helpful when the other party needs guidance to draw out related information.

Reflection question

Reflection questions are those after-event thoughts. They seek to learn from an experience or encounter. Example "After this incident, what would you have done otherwise?" The aim is to solicit and collect personal learnings and opinions from an event.

Probing question

Probing questions try to dig out more facts. Example "What did you do before you switch on the electrical power?" Commonly used for detective and investigative works where facts and information are not given voluntarily nor willingly. The party may have something they want to hide.

Hypothetical question

Hypothetical questions are those that build up speculative scenarios. Example "Could you have left the engine running and it got overheated?" The facts may not be available, or no one has them. These questions build-up likely scenarios in an attempt to establish some credible data to work upon.

Chapter 11

Resolve Conflict for Team Effectiveness

Charles and Robert have been working as a delivery team for "Top Chocolates" for the last six months. They are assigned a region with 65 supermarkets. Their job is to ensure that these supermarkets are well stocked up with the company's 16 varieties of chocolate products. This may include monitoring their stock levels, stacking up and ensuring pleasant visual displays.

Initially it was pleasant working together. They appreciated each other's working attitude; relax and yet hard working, able to get the job done efficiently and of a high standard. They enjoyed a good working relationship and were a great team. Recently, however, they seemed to be rather strained. Even supervisors from some of the supermarkets could feel it. Well, as they enjoyed a good working relationship, Robert began to share some personal and family matters with Charles. Charles might have casually shared these with other colleagues without any ill thought. Robert felt betrayed when he got to know that his personal matters were shared and discussed among other colleagues. He got angry with Charles, and began guarded against him that subsequently led to antagonistic reactions.

Charles and Robert started well but ended up in a conflict situation. Conflict can arise in a team due to many reasons. Knowing the factors contributing to, and recognising the stages of conflict development can help minimise or resolve conflict in a team.

What is Conflict

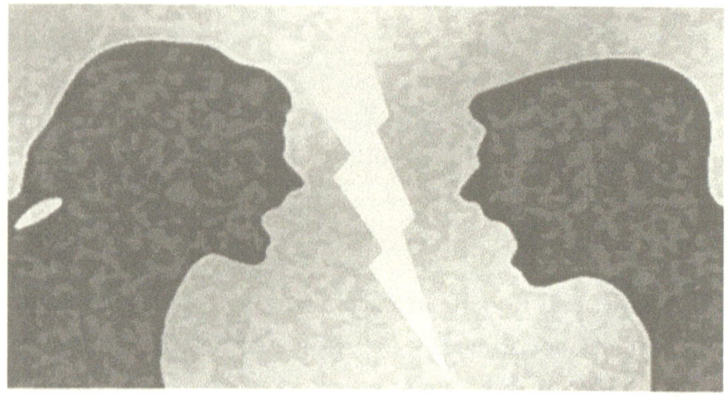

Conflict is a serious disagreement about something between two parties that have yet to reach an agreement of resolution. Its occurrence threatens the team's harmony, and prolong existence causes disunity and eventual destruction. Disagreement is not a conflict. Disagreement is a situation in which two parties have different opinions, or an inability to agree. By itself, disagreement may not lead to an adverse consequence. Disagreement is at times encouraged. For example during a brainstorming session where critics on ideas are welcomed. However, disagreement can escalate to a conflict that ends up with unintended consequences when both parties insist that the other party is wrong.

Stages of Conflict Development

Conflict arises due to many factors. Some of which relate to personalities, while others influence by the environment. Personality factors could include the style of doing things, personal value, and different perceptions of an issue. Environmental factors could include limiting resources, conflicting goals or differing priorities. One or a combination of these factors could easily stage a conflict.

Conflict usually escalates to levels of seriousness. Recognizing the stages of conflict development helps us address and arrest conflict before it escalates to the next stage. It is easier to intervene and resolve conflict at the early stages. However these early stages are not easy to detect, but rather convenient to ignore and simpler to overlook. Professional help will be required when conflict escalates to the crisis stage. Let's take a look at the stages of conflict development starting from the early ones.

Discomfort

This is probably the earliest stage of conflict development. Parties begin to notice tension or become aware of a disagreement. This is not recognized as a problem, it is usually ignored, and nothing or little is said or done about it. At this stage, parties concerned are able to look at it objectively and seek common ground. Cooperation rules.

Some causes of discomfort could be mannerism, behavior or speech. Respective examples could be swiping at handphones while spoken to (mannerism), physical touching the other party during a conversation (behavior), or using certain swear words (speech). The other party may not be comfortable with these due to personal value or culture. These mismatches cause discomfort.

Incident

The tension or discomfort escalates to this stage when both parties stick obstinately to their own point of view. Negative meaning events or incidents begin to occur. Tensions build up that lead to mistrust and a problem is recognized. Any conversation is used to convince or win over the opposing side. Communication breaks down as no one is listening. This is becoming more of a debate of the wits and battle of opinion. Cooperation gives way to competition.

Continue with one example from the previous point; the swiping of handphone while spoken to. The party swiping on the phone insists that he needs only to use his ears to listen. He does not need his eyes to help him listen to the message. The other party is very sure that one cannot multi task effectively. Sometimes these arguments would be a short conversation, other times they could be more involved. Often they are not conclusive nor would they end with an agreement.

Misunderstandings

Both parties begin to avoid each other as the incidents do not end well nor pleasant. The intent of this avoidance was to reduce unpleasant incidents. However non-communication easily leads to mutual suspicion. Allowing this suspicion to fester on leads to misunderstanding, and it quickly develops to the next stage.

The party using the handphone began to feel unfairly pick upon all the time, while the other party begins to grumble that he is being rude and irresponsible. Both sides refuse to talk and are becoming convinced of their respective suspicion.

Tension

Tensions arise as suspicion and mistrust develop. Both parties get negative and loose hope of any compromise solution. Each side may be becoming hostile toward the other.

The party using the handphone is now convinced that the other party has a bone to pick and begins to defend his right to use the phone vigorously. The other party feels the phone guy is being unreasonable, irrational and rude, besides being irresponsible. He may even begin to champion against the use of handphone in work.

Crisis

The discomfort has gone a complete round and come to the crisis stage. Both parties make no attempt to conceal their hostility. They will not talk to nor interact with the other party. They begin to identify and call the other party with negative terms and names. They may even begin to recruit members to join their respective groups. This has developed into a full-blown conflict.

At this stage, they need external help to resolve the situation. A non-interested or professional third party may need to come in to go through the conflict resolution process.

Stages of Conflict Development

Steps to Conflict Resolution

For the conflict resolution to be meaningful and fruitful, both parties need to recognise and acknowledge that there is a conflict, and to express a willingness and desire to work toward a common resolution.

Step 1: Clarify the disagreement

Begin the conflict resolution process by obtaining as much information as possible from both parties by asking questions until each side understands the other's point of view. Get both parties to agree to hear out completely from each other without interrupting. Assure them that each party will be given enough time to tell their stories fully.

The aim is to establish all facts, avoid and remove emotions, and clarify the disagreement.

Step 2: Establish a common goal for both parties

With all the information fully laid out, find a commonality from both sides, and discuss what each party would like to see happen as the final outcome.

For example both involved parties would like to see an enjoyable working environment where all parties are perceived to be kind, responsible and respectful.

Step 3: Discuss ways to meet the common goal

With the established common goal in view, next brainstorm different possible and acceptable approaches to meet the goal. Do not be concern about finding and deciding the perfect plan at this stage. The aim is to generate more than 2 possible approaches to the goal.

Examples may include signing workers up for communication classes to help them understand the processes for effective communication, or some bonding sessions for working team, or set aside time for team building sessions. Maybe a session on understanding and respecting differences could be helpful?

Step 4: Determine the barriers to the common goal

Determine what can and cannot be changed, and discuss ways to get around those roadblocks. The aim is to allow both parties to explore various ideas, discuss their advantages and understand the challenges. The process helps both parties to appreciate the gravity of the conflict, and increase the desire to resolve it.

Some barriers to the common goal could be personal value like punctuality, working condition that does not allow interaction among workers.

Step 5: Agree on the best way to resolve the conflict

When the common goal is identified and agreed upon, the possible acceptable approaches discussed, and their challenges understood, this is the time to agree on the best way to resolve the conflict. Realise that the best way to resolve the conflict could be a combination of approaches discussed in step 3. Work out a progress monitoring plan and follow-up sessions.

Both parties must agree and accept the choice to resolve the conflict.

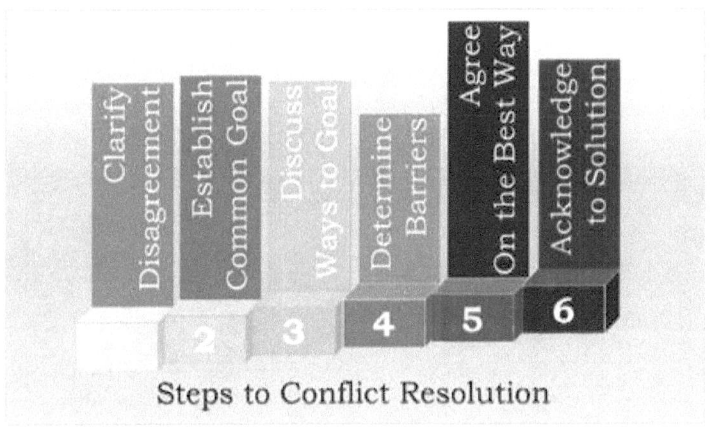

Steps to Conflict Resolution

Step 6: Acknowledge the agreed solution and each party's responsibilities in the resolution

Get both parties to acknowledge a win-win situation. Ensure the responsibility each party has to maintain for the solution to work is understood, agreed upon and accepted by both parties. Both parties must commit to this resolution, ensuring that this conflict does not arise again.

Methods of Conflict Resolution

Thomas and Kilmann identified a conflict-handling grid comprised of five conflict management styles based on two dimensions: assertiveness and cooperativeness. Assertiveness refers to the motivation of an individual to achieve his/her own goals or outcomes. Cooperativeness assesses the willingness to allow the other party to achieve its goals or outcomes. These 2 factors plot onto a matrix of 5 styles: namely Avoiding, Competing, Accommodating, Compromising and Collaborating. Any of the five conflict resolution styles might be the appropriate one base on circumstances and the personalities of the individual involve.

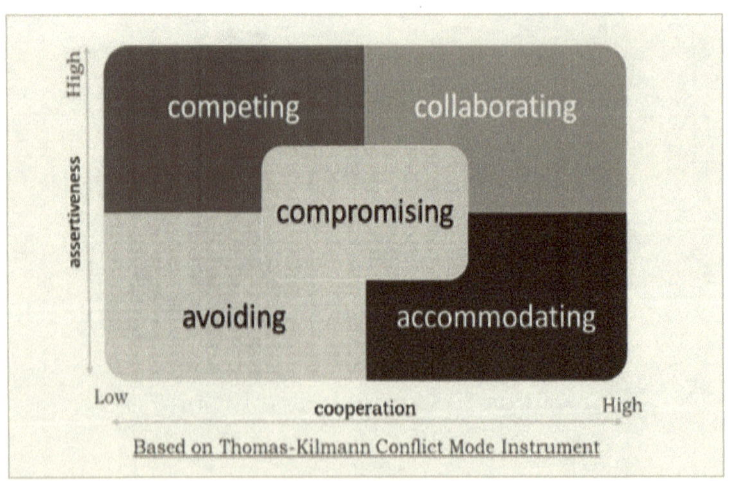

Conflict Resolution Styles

Avoiding

This is a style where both assertiveness and cooperativeness are low. Both parties do not view their personal agenda as high, nor do they feel any need to cater to others' needs. The incident or discomfort is perceived to be trivial and is never really addressed or resolved. This could be an appropriate style for trivial matters, or when there is no chance of winning or when disruption would be very costly.

An example could be a supervisor is not cooperative in helping his subordinates to achieve their personal goals, nor is he aggressively pursuing his preferred outcomes. The conflict arises as the supervisor has team targets to achieve, and is also responsible to upgrade his team members. Avoiding making any decision has served him well so far.

Competing

Competing style is known as the win-lose approach where the assertiveness is high and cooperativeness is low. The supervisor is aggressively pursuing his goal, and not cooperative in helping individuals to achieve their goals. This is an appropriate style when quick, decisive action is needed, such as during emergencies.

For example when there is a fire outbreak, the supervisor orders all staff to clear the kitchen immediately, leaving whatever they are doing on the table. The supervisor needs to make the call, maybe following some SOPs, there is no room to consider if any individual's work is important.

Accommodating

Accommodating style is known as the lose-win approach where the assertiveness is low and the cooperativeness is high. The supervisor is not aggressively pursuing his preferred outcomes, but instead is cooperative in helping individuals to achieve their goals. This style is appropriate when an issue is more important to one party than the other.

An example is when an employee has to take time off to attend classes for an upgrading program he is pursuing. While the supervisor has team goals to achieve and projects to accomplish, he chooses to help the employee achieve his goal. The supervisor may need to arrange some work-from-home working for that employee instead.

Compromising

Compromising approach is referred to as the bargaining or trading approach. The assertiveness and cooperativeness levels are both moderate, and both parties have about equal power. This could be an appropriate approach when a temporary, timely solution is needed.

An example could be when two sport teams need to prepare for national competitions. Both the basketball team and the floorball team are preparing for the inter-school game. Their training courts are on the same spot in the multi-purpose hall. An arrangement could be made that each take an alternate day or alternating time slot for their respective training.

Collaborating

Collaborating style is known as the win-win approach where both assertiveness and cooperativeness are high. Both parties are working toward achieving the goals and desired outcomes for all parties. This style may be appropriate for a complex situation and creative ideas are required.

An example could be a combined product launch for the sales and the product development teams. Each team may have their own direction and goal which are not aligned or even conflicting with the other. You see, sales guys just want to clock in the figures, and product development guys take pride only in designing the best product. For this combine launch, they have to explore and work out a strategy where both their goals aligning and benefits complimenting. They would need to collaborate to discover each other strengths and capabilities, and seek to fulfill one another's goal and target.

Of the five conflict resolution styles, only a collaborating strategy seeks a win-win outcome. The rest of the other four styles fall into a win-lose strategy. While the win-win strategy has gained popularity with most recent management consultants and practitioners, the other four win-lose styles have their places too. Which strategy to use depend on the specific situation, the party personality style, the desired outcome, and the time available. For example in a situation where two suppliers are bidding for a project, a competing strategy would be appropriate. You can't seek a win-win situation here as there will be a winner (the one who gets the project) and the losers (the rest who don't get the project).

What other situations can you think of where the other strategies would be appropriate?

Snapshot Summary for Up My Personal Effectiveness

A quick read to the Snapshot for Up My Personal Effectiveness. A fundamental belief and assumption of this book are that everyone wants to be able to make positive contributions and impacts to personal and team lives.

One important shift is to develop a success and resilience mindset, that is, everyone is of great value and has the resources to make positive contributions. This is covered in Part One. The tool-sets that could help one to up his personal effectiveness are discussed in Part Three. Skill-sets required to do the same are discussed in Part Four. With the learning from these 3 parts, an action plan can then be developed. This is covered in Part Two.

All activities up to this point are the cognitive learning and planning phases. The next step changes gear into the execution phase.

The next critical phase to Up My Personal Effectiveness is to execute the action plan. The importance of this phase cannot be understated. Many great plans were jeopardised at this stage due to failure or non-execution of the plan. Be sure to carry through this phase. The cycle of implementing, monitoring, reflecting and re-aligning the action plan will ensure personal successes and team victories. While these are the processes of project management and are outside the scope of this book, a short introduction to a powerful project management tool (Gantt Chart) is discussed in Chapter 4.

I wish you every success to Up My Personal Effectiveness journey!

APPENDIX A: PLANNING TEMPLATES

Specific	
Measurable	
Attainable	
Realistic	
Time-based	
SMART Goals	

SMART Goal Planning

SWOT Analysis

SOAR Analysis

Gantt Chart
Activities
Jan
Feb
Mar
Apr
May
Jun

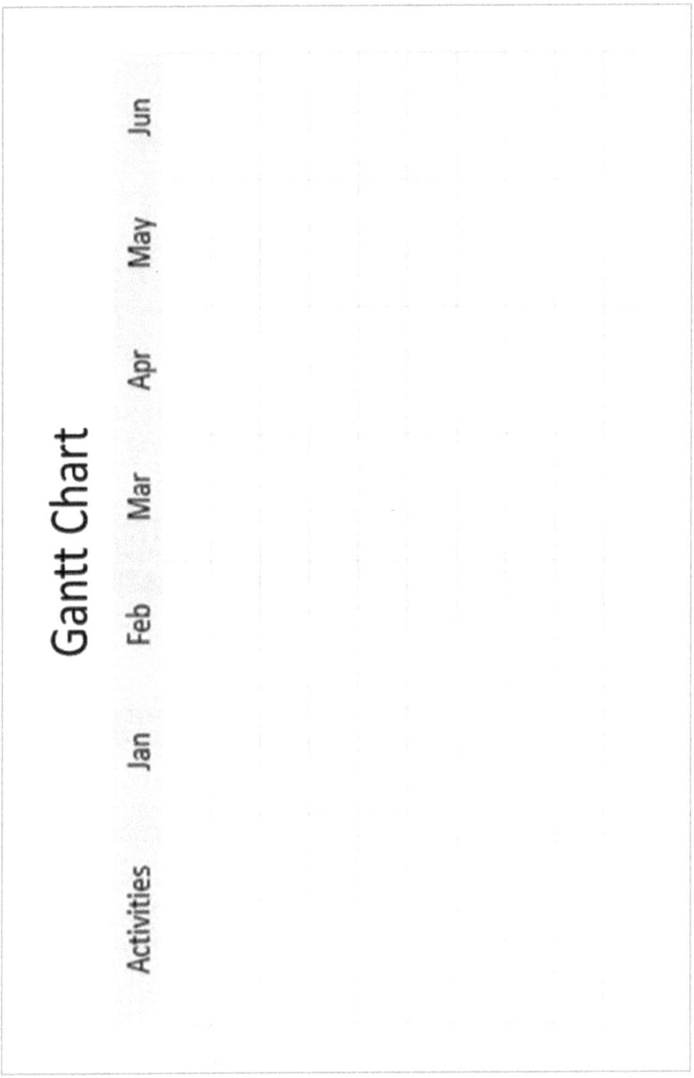

Up My Core Skills Series

This book is a part of Up My Core Skills Series. Core Skills refer to essential skills that are required throughout one's life stages, and they transpire across functions, industries, and roles. They are non-static and evolve along the way. So must you.

This book is also available in e-formats on Amazon Kindle and PDF versions. It is presented as 4 parts eBook:

Part One: Understand Personal Effectiveness

Part Two: Develop Action Plan

Part Three: Manage Self Effectively

Part Four: Work With Others

You may purchase the e-format copies from Amazon Kindle bookstore, or check them out at www.onepurpletree.com

References

http://www.referenceforbusiness.com/management/Comp-De/Conflict-Management-and-Negotiation.html#ixzz5B8058Zu3

http://extension.wsu.edu/wallawalla/wp-content/uploads/sites/26/2016/08/The-big-book-of-Conflict-Resolution-Games.pdf

http://www.dchs.nhs.uk/assets/public/dchs/dchs_staff_zone/TOF/mecc/Recognising_stress_in_yourself_-_signs_and_syptoms_-_amended_V2.pdf

http://www.doc.wa.gov/docs/publications/fact-sheets/16-008-F2.pdf

http://www.ocds.info/conference/ConflictResolution.pdf

http://www.referenceforbusiness.com/management/Comp-De/Conflict-Management-and-Negotiation.html#ixzz5B8058Zu3

https://greatist.com/grow/motivation-tips-that-work#tools

https://www.accipio.com/eleadership/mod/wiki/view.php?id=1858

https://www.helpguide.org/articles/relationships-communication/effective-communication.htm

https://www.helpguide.org/articles/stress/stress-symptoms-signs-and-causes.htm

https://www.skillsyouneed.com/ps/self-motivation.html

https://www.wikihow.com/Be-Self-Motivated

ABOUT THE AUTHOR

Jonathan facilitates learning sessions for adults discovering topics on core skills. These including personal effectiveness, tribe building, effective communication, resilience and seeking significance. His approaches are largely influenced by his engineering disciplines and 25 years of sales experiences – methodical, processes, personable and outcome-focused. He is fascinated by the immense potential of nature's twin gifts: People and Land. Jonathan enjoys jogging, reading and chocolate.

You can contact Jonathan at jonathan@onepurpletree.com

www.onepurpletree.com